WISDOM FROM

THE PROVERBS

WISDOM FROM
THE PROVERBS

A 40-DAY
DEVOTIONAL JOURNEY

PETER HORROBIN

Chosen

a division of Baker Publishing Group
Minneapolis, Minnesota

© 2019 by Peter Horrobin

Published by Chosen Books
11400 Hampshire Avenue South
Bloomington, Minnesota 55438
www.chosenbooks.com

Chosen Books is a division of
Baker Publishing Group, Grand Rapids, Michigan

Printed in the United States of America

Library of Congress Cataloging-in-Publication Data
Names: Horrobin, Peter J. (Peter James), author.
Title: Wisdom from the Proverbs : a 40-day devotional journey / Peter Horrobin.
Description: Bloomington : Chosen Books, 2019. | Originally published under the title
    Wisdom from the Proverbs, A 40-Day Devotional Journey, by Sovereign World Ltd,
    Ellel Ministries International, Ellel, Lancaster, Lancashire, LA2 0HN, United Kingdom—
    Title verso.
Identifiers: LCCN 2019024906 | ISBN 9780800799441 (paperback) | ISBN 9781493420407
    (ebook)
Subjects: LCSH: Bible. Proverbs—Devotional literature.
Classification: LCC BS1465.54 .H67 2019 | DDC 242/.5—dc23
LC record available at https://lccn.loc.gov/2019024906

Unless otherwise noted, Scripture quotations are from the HOLY BIBLE, NEW INTERNATIONAL VERSION. Copyright © 1973, 1978, 1984 International Bible Society. Used by permission of Zondervan.

Scripture quotations marked KJV are from the King James Version of the Bible.

Cover design by Studio Gearbox

19 20 21 22 23 24 25   7 6 5 4 3 2 1

CONTENTS

INTRODUCTION

Information and wisdom are very different. Someone could be the most knowledgeable person in the world but be seriously deficient in wisdom and have little understanding of what it means to live a godly life. And another person may be relatively unlearned and yet be able to exercise profound wisdom in the decisions that he or she has to make on life's journey.

It is not unusual to read the achievements of very clever people, and then discover that their private lives are an absolute disaster, punctuated with the consequences of unwise decisions, broken relationships and financial loss. The media is never slow to profile the mistakes of the rich and famous.

Young people idolize the stars of the music, entertainment and sporting worlds. But the private lives of their heroes are rarely steeped in godliness. Beneath the veneer of success and popularity can lie a maelstrom of sinful behavior. It is no surprise, therefore, that, when they grow up, their behavior replicates that of the people they follow.

When Solomon succeeded his father, David, to the throne of Israel, he went up to Gibeon and stood before the Tabernacle inquiring of the Lord. The Lord said to him, "Ask for whatever you want me to give you" (2 Chronicles 1:7). And because Solomon asked for knowledge and wisdom, and not riches and wealth, the Lord said He would give him both. Solomon became renowned for both his wisdom and his wealth, exceeding that of any king before or since.

It is generally understood that the wisdom Solomon was blessed with was nothing less than the Spirit of God speaking through him. It was a gift of God. We also read about this gift of God in James 1:5, which says, "If any of you lacks wisdom, he should ask God, who gives generously to all without finding fault, and it will be given to him."

Because of the knowledge and wisdom that God gave Solomon, his reign was extraordinarily successful. He prospered. And not only did he prosper, but he was privileged with the task of building the Temple that his father had dreamed of. On a second occasion, after the Temple was built, Solomon was blessed with another direct encounter with the Lord, who appeared to him at night and said, "I have heard your prayer and have chosen this place for myself as a temple for sacrifices" (2 Chronicles 7:12). And then God said, "If my people, who are called by my name, will humble themselves and pray and seek my face and turn from their wicked ways, then will I hear from heaven and will forgive their sin and will heal their land" (verse 14).

This is an extraordinary promise rich in meaning—both for the nation of Israel and for God's people of all generations. For us now, I have seen

God's promise of healing and restoration, subsequent to humble repentance, fulfilled a thousand times over in the lives of people of all nations and cultures. God loves to honor His promises. Peter reminds his readers of this divine principle when he says, "Humble yourselves, therefore, under God's mighty hand, that he may lift you up in due time" (1 Peter 5:6).

Which brings us to the book of Proverbs. Within the confines of these 31 chapters, God has condensed and placed the wisdom that was received as a gift by Solomon. What Solomon wrote down in chapter after chapter of pithy, expressive, dynamic and challenging sayings is like a bottle of vitamin pills for the soul. But in order to know the blessing that God planned for His people through their use, we have to humble ourselves (that means deal with our pride) and let God speak to our hearts.

For this devotional, I have selected forty of these sayings, which embody life-transforming spiritual principles, as a journey of spiritual understanding that will speak to your heart. But for the maximum blessing and benefit, the "vitamin pills" have to be taken. I encourage you to set out on this journey with an open heart toward the Lord, praying that He will speak into your life and bring healing and restoration to your soul as you draw on the wisdom God has placed within the Proverbs to build you up in Him.

How to Use This Book

This book has been laid out as a forty-step journey of faith. It was designed to be read little by little, one day at a time. Before you begin to read each day's Scripture and the devotional reading, spend a few moments in prayer—lay aside all the concerns of the moment and ask the Holy Spirit to open God's Word to you and to minister His truth into your inner being.

Then read the Scripture for the day—not once, but two or three times, allowing God to speak to you personally through it. Next, read the devotional with an open heart, asking God to show you how the things that are said can relate to events and circumstances in your own life. You may find it helpful to read the devotional through again.

At the end of each devotional is a suggested prayer that will help you anchor the daily truths into the reality of your own life. But I would encourage you to pray more personally as well, applying to your own situation whatever God has said to you through the devotional.

Finally, there is a space for you to make your own personal comments about the Scripture and the devotional and keep a record of what God says to you. It has always been a huge encouragement to me to look back at the things that God has said or done in the past and track the record of God's hand on my life.

I pray that this little book will be a rich blessing to you, and that as you move on with God, you will know His presence and empowerment day by day.

Day 1

ON WHAT ARE YOU LEANING?

Trust in the LORD with all your heart and lean not on your own understanding; in all your ways acknowledge him, and he will make your paths straight.

Proverbs 3:5–6

The Leaning Tower of Pisa is unstable. When people first see the structure they are amazed that it is still standing. An enormous amount of careful engineering has been necessary to preserve this iconic structure that attracts tourists from all over the world. It is a massive money earner for Italy.

But it is not what the architect intended! It was meant to be upright. It leans because the ground on which it was built is too soft on one side of the structure. It is quite literally leaning according to its own understanding of weight, pressure and gravity.

If the ground on which we build our lives is not firm, then we, too, will lean according to our own understanding and go our own way. It is absolutely vital that we follow the advice of our Scripture for today and trust in the Lord. Only He knows everything about us and our circumstances, and only He is able to direct our steps according to His plans and purposes for our lives.

This is how our devotional journey should begin—by humbling ourselves and choosing to trust that God's Word and His teaching are more important and much more reliable than our own ideas and inclinations.

When we begin to trust our own understanding without reference to the God who made and loves us, it will be as if the ground beneath our feet begins to shift. Before long, our lives will become unstable; they will no longer be upright. That is why there are such extremes of ungodliness in society. And just as the cost of propping up the Leaning Tower of Pisa has been extensive, so is the personal and societal cost when people ignore God's Word and follow their own inclinations. Trying to correct lives that have gone off course, without God, is a never-ending, never-succeeding roundabout of human effort without godly gain.

To trust in the Lord means to depend on Him totally and not on our own seemingly good, but ungodly, ideas. Our Scripture stresses that we should trust Him with *all* of our hearts—not just a "religious bit" that we are happy for Him to have, provided we can keep hold of the rest. Some of the kings of Israel and Judah were less than wholehearted in their service to the Lord—and as a result their lives and reigns did not end well.

God's promises to those who do trust Him wholeheartedly, meaning with all of their hearts, are many and wonderful—including this one, that He will help us continue in a good and right direction. Or, as I learned it in the King James Version, "He shall direct thy paths."

Many are the times when I have sensed God bringing correction into my life so that the path I am walking on will remain straight. And many are the times when I have sensed Him directing my paths so that I may know His will for the next stage of my life. I am grateful to God for His wisdom—it is beyond human understanding.

Help me, Lord, to trust You at all times and to look for Your clear direction in my life. I pray that You will direct my steps so that the paths I walk on will be those You have prepared for me. In Jesus' name, Amen.

DAY 1

Day 2

WALKING IN THE PLANS AND PURPOSES OF GOD

Many are the plans in a man's heart, but it is the LORD's purpose that prevails.

Proverbs 19:21

God has a plan and a purpose for each one of our lives. We may have lots of ideas about what we would like to do with the years that stretch before us, but our ideas need to be tested and submitted to the great Planner. One of the greatest of the old hymns, "Guide Me, O Thou Great Redeemer" by William Williams, expresses powerfully what should be the desire of our hearts:

> Guide me, O Thou great Redeemer,
> Pilgrim through this barren land;
> I am weak, but Thou art mighty,
> Hold me with Thy pow'rful hand.

It does not matter whether we still have most of our lives to live or are wondering if the year ahead might be our last; God still has a strategy and a plan for us. However many years there may be in store, we still have a choice as to how we will fill our time.

God has given each of us free will. But if our free will is not gladly surrendered to His purposes for our lives, we could easily miss out on His best for us. We could also find ourselves in danger of coming up against the purposes of God, which, as our Scripture indicates, will prevail. It is far better to be flowing in the will and purposes of God than to discover at a later time that we have been going in a direction opposite to God's plan for our lives.

God is Creator—and we are made in His image and likeness. That means we are creative also. He rejoices to inspire our own creativity and to fill our minds with plans that will be a blessing to us personally and that will be purposeful in His Kingdom.

I have found on many occasions that when we walk in fellowship with and obedience to God, He gives us vision. And, further, He opens the way ahead so that the vision He has given becomes His purpose for us.

You really matter to God. He loves you unconditionally. He does not condemn you because of mistakes in the past but wants to forgive you, heal you from their consequences and equip you for the days ahead. He wants only His best for you. There are many strands to each one of our lives; when God weaves those strands together, He creates a beautiful tapestry.

Sometimes it is the strand of little consequence at the time that proves to be of great significance in later years. We cannot avoid having to live in a fallen world that has rejected the God who made it. And we may be going through tough times as a result, but no matter how difficult the journey may be, God has assured us that He will be with us every step of the way.

Thank You, Jesus, for being my Redeemer and for Your commitment to being my Guide through life. Forgive me, Lord, when I have tried to do things that were not Your best for me. Help me, Lord, to see how precious it is to be Your representative in working out Your purposes. In Jesus' name, Amen.

DAY 2

Day 3

HONORING THE LORD

Honor the LORD with your wealth, with the firstfruits of all your crops; then your barns will be filled to overflowing, and your vats will brim over with new wine.

Proverbs 3:9–10

There are many scientific laws governing the physical universe in which we live. Gravity, for example, keeps our feet firmly on the ground and makes things feel heavy. If you drop something, it will always fall downward. This is the fundamental law that holds our universe together, keeps planet earth in place going around the sun and keeps the moon in place going around the earth. We all know the importance of respecting these physical laws and are careful not to fall off the edge of a building or a cliff, for we know that if we do, we will come to harm.

In addition to all the physical laws that scientists have discovered, there are spiritual laws within God's spiritual universe. God has told us about these in His Word. If we ignore these spiritual laws, then there will also be consequences.

Knowledge of God's spiritual laws is intended to be a blessing for us. If, for instance, we choose to do those things that God has told us not to do, such as worship idols or commit adultery, then we are putting ourselves outside of God's protection—and that is dangerous. It is like trying to defy gravity by stepping off the edge of a cliff.

If we fail to do the things that God has told us to do, such as honoring our parents, then we will miss out on the many blessings that result. Our Scripture for today highlights one of those spiritual laws through which God wants to bless us: honoring the Lord with our wealth.

To honor God means to worship Him. We worship by our love and obedience to Him, by giving Him our time, by listening to His voice, by doing those things that please Him, by singing His praises. And one of the spiritual laws that is intrinsic to our relationship with God is that when we honor Him, He chooses to bless us. Deuteronomy 28:1–14 shows us some of the many ways God chose to bless His people when they honored Him with their obedience.

An important part of honoring God is to give to Him the firstfruits of whatever He leads us to do—to bring to Him our tithes and offerings and to give with thankful hearts when the Lord prompts us to share with others what He has given us. That is worship. And as we worship by responding to the promptings of the Holy Spirit to give, the Lord chooses to pour back upon us His blessings, in His way and in His time.

We do not give to God so that we will get a reward—that is the selfish deception of what is sometimes called the "prosperity Gospel." But when we give to Him because we love Him and want to worship Him, then God has promised that we will know His blessings in our lives—and we can trust His Word. For, as Paul expressed it so powerfully, "My God will meet all your needs according to his glorious riches in Christ Jesus" (Philippians 4:19).

Thank You, Lord, for the amazing promises that are in Your Word. Forgive me, Lord, for the times when I have withheld from You my worship of giving. Help me, I pray, to learn how to honor You with everything You have given me, so that my giving may be a blessing to others and to You. In Jesus' name, Amen.

DAY 3

Day 4

LEARNING HOW TO LIVE LONGER

"The fear of the LORD is the beginning of wisdom, and knowledge of the Holy One is understanding. For through me your days will be many, and years will be added to your life."

Proverbs 9:10–11

Living longer is the dream of most people, but not many in today's world discover one of the most precious keys to a long life, which is found in Scripture. And the reason they fail to find it is because they are ignorant of what God says in His Word.

Holy fear of a holy God is the first pillar of truth from these verses, and it is critical for life. If we learn to live in awe of and have reverence for the God who loves us so much, then we are choosing to live in holy fear. That does not mean we will be afraid of Him, for there is no reason why we should fear love. But, as a result, we will want to do what is right and will not want to do those things that grieve Him by stepping off His pathway for our lives.

But the second pillar—knowledge of the Holy One—is equally important. Knowing everything we can discover from God's Word about His nature and character will give us an understanding of God and His ways, and will help us fulfill His purposes for our lives. This is one of the prime reasons why we need to feed our spirits daily by reading the Bible, for it is here that we learn about Him.

People who know me, because they have worked with me in Ellel Ministries for many years, have come to understand how I think and what I would do in many different circumstances. As a result, I have complete confidence and trust in them and the way they run the different Ellel centers around the world. If they did not know me, they would not understand the heart of the ministry and know what to do in each situation. Either they would have to get in touch with me constantly to ask for direction or they would make mistakes, because they would be acting without understanding of my heart or the way God has led us to serve Him in the ministry.

In just the same way, we need to get to know the heart of God. Once we have His heart and He has ours, we can move forward in faith and trust, confident that He will lead us.

And when we are doing those things that please Him, we can be confident that we will not be doing those things that could have the effect of shortening our lives. This is easy to understand when you see the medical statistics about the shortened life expectancy of those who are addicted to drugs or who catch sexually transmitted diseases through promiscuous sexual relationships. There is plenty of evidence in the daily news of our nation that living an ungodly life can have a serious life-shortening effect.

Living a holy life in the fear of God is not living a dull life. It is the most challenging and exciting life imaginable. And God promises to add years to our lives when we understand and walk in His ways.

Thank You, Lord, for the wonderful promises we find in Your Word. Help me to get to know You better. I ask that Your Holy Spirit will fill me day by day with His power to strengthen me against temptation and enable me to be a blessing to You and to others. In Jesus' name, Amen.

DAY 4

Day 5

MONEY—SERVANT OR IDOL?

Whoever trusts in his riches will fall, but the righteous will thrive like a green leaf.

Proverbs 11:28

The book of Proverbs has lots to say about the three most dangerous temptations: money, sex and power. These temptations are a constant threat, even to believers, no matter how far they have run in their personal races of life.

Money is one of life's essentials. Without it we cannot buy necessities such as food, clothing and shelter. With it almost everything we could ever want or dream of becomes possible. Whenever there is a great natural disaster our television screens are full of appeals—what for? For money. With money the charitable agencies can supply the needs of suffering people.

Scripture encourages us to consider that everything we have belongs to God—and to be generous toward those in need. But because money can buy anything, wanting more can be a dangerous temptation. Money can buy good things, but it can also be used for purposes that will take our eyes off God, lead us astray and consume our souls.

There is nothing that can so quickly grow a spiritual cataract over our eyes as greed. It can have the effect of blinding us so that we cannot see the deceptive traps we may be falling into. And then, when we have acquired a lot of money, fear takes hold. Why? Because any time we put our trust in money as the means of doing whatever we want, we are no longer trusting God to be our provider (Jehovah-Jireh); we are trusting in what has become an idol in our hearts. And idolatry is driven by fear rather than love.

The fear of not having enough makes people desperate to protect what they have. And the fear of losing it can turn the rich from generous givers into the meanest of people, as portrayed by Ebenezer Scrooge in Charles Dickens's amazing novel *A Christmas Carol*. This character gave birth to a new word in the English language—a *scrooge*: a mean, miserly and unhappy person, even though rich in this world's goods.

Those who depend on their riches are shortsighted. As today's Scripture tells us, those who trust in riches will fall. Proverbs 27:24 adds to this: "Riches do not endure forever." When the Scriptures talk about not lasting forever, they are contrasting the perspective of time and eternity. Earthly wealth can run out, and it has no eternal value.

We may die as rich people, but where is the treasure of our hearts located? If it is in the wealth we are leaving behind, we have problems, as

Jesus explained in His parable of the rich farmer in Luke 12:13–21. The man wanted to build bigger barns in which he could store all his grain and all his goods, so that he could then "take life easy; eat, drink and be merry."

But God's assessment of this man's objectives was very different. The man had been blinded by his riches to eternal truths. In the story God said to him, "You fool! This very night your life will be demanded from you. Then who will get what you have prepared for yourself?"

Jesus concluded, "This is how it will be with anyone who stores up things for himself but is not rich toward God."

Money can be a means of huge provision and blessing. But it can also be a self-destructive trap. If this is an area of temptation for you, I pray that you will learn to take your eyes off what you have here in "earth time" and focus on what you can take with you into eternity: "For where your treasure is, there your heart will be also" (Matthew 6:21). When we are living righteous lives with the right focus in our hearts, we will, as our verse tells us, thrive—without the need to be trusting in riches, for they will fall.

Help me, Lord, to value Your provision and to trust You for all I need. Forgive me, Lord, for the times when I have taken my eyes off You and trusted in my possessions instead of You. Give me Your wisdom to have a right balance in my life, to be generous with what You have given me and to keep my focus on You—the treasure of my heart. In Jesus' name, Amen.

DAY 5

Day 6

SATAN'S TRAP

For a man's ways are in full view of the LORD, and he examines all his paths. The evil deeds of a wicked man ensnare him; the cords of his sin hold him fast.

Proverbs 5:21–22

The book of Proverbs is full of amazing wisdom to help guide the believer along the road of life and avoid Satan's pitfalls. Almost three whole chapters are devoted to the consequences of sexual sin. This must, therefore, be a very serious issue if God's warnings against sexual sin and adultery have such prominence.

Proverbs is not the only place in the Bible where the warnings are so specific. In Paul's letter to the Galatians, for example, he listed sexual immorality among the sins people commit that could disinherit them from the Kingdom of God (see 5:19–21). To the Ephesians he said, "Among you there must not be even a hint of sexual immorality" (5:3). And, of course, Jesus Himself said that "anyone who looks at a woman lustfully has already committed adultery with her in his heart" (Matthew 5:28), teaching us that lust of the eyes precedes the lustful fulfillment of a wrong physical relationship. And Paul reminded believers, "If you think you are standing firm, be careful that you don't fall!" (1 Corinthians 10:12).

So, why is sexual sin so dangerous that it merits so many scriptural warnings, in addition to the seventh Commandment not to commit adultery? The heart of the answer lies in our Scripture for today, which comes at the end of Proverbs 5, and which is headed in my Bible, "Warning Against Adultery." In 1 Corinthians 6:18 Paul warned believers to "flee from sexual immorality. All other sins a man commits are outside his body, but he who sins sexually sins against his own body." In these verses we have an important answer to the question displaying enormous wisdom, which, if followed, can be truly lifesaving.

When a man and a woman enter into marriage and, thereby, into a godly sexual relationship, they are entering into a covenantal, God-ordained union by which the man and the woman become one with and part of each other. A similar, but ungodly, union also takes place when a sexual relationship occurs outside of marriage. But this time, instead of it being a union that is blessed by God, it is sinful bondage.

This is because, as our Scripture says, the cords of such sin hold a person fast. That individual is now tied to another in a union that God did not intend and that He cannot bless. Not only, therefore, is the sin against God, it is, as Paul said, a sin against one's own body. Joining the body, indeed one's whole being, with someone else has the result of giving that person spiritual access to and influence over one's whole identity—a privilege that God had reserved for a husband-wife relationship.

Every time people enter into ungodly sexual relationships, something of their own identity is given away to their sexual partners, and they in turn receive something of the identity of their partners. No wonder Proverbs describes sexual sin as cords that hold us fast. And Proverbs 6:32 says: "A man who commits adultery lacks judgment; whoever does so destroys himself." The pleasure may be for a moment, but it is like pressing a self-destruct button to one's own identity.

Praise God that there is a way out of the mess. In 1 Corinthians 6 Paul lists many of the sexual sins people can commit, but in verse 11 he states the unequivocal good news that "that is what some of you were. But you were washed, you were sanctified, you were justified in the name of the Lord Jesus Christ and by the Spirit of our God." He is simply stating the wonderful Gospel truth that where there is true repentance, there can be forgiveness and healing—even from the consequences of sexual sin.

Thank You, Lord, that Your Word warns us of the dangers of sexual sin. I ask You, Lord, to forgive me and cleanse me from every bit of sexual uncleanness in my life. And where there have been wrong relationships, I ask you to break the cords of bondage, so that I might be free to serve You, unimpeded by the consequences of my sin. In Jesus' name, Amen.

DAY 6

Day 7

LAZINESS, WORK AND WEALTH

Lazy hands make a man poor, but diligent hands bring wealth. He who gathers crops in summer is a wise son, but he who sleeps during harvest is a disgraceful son.

Proverbs 10:4-5

I was recently reading about a man who, at the age of sixty, heard that he might have a terminal condition. Instead of bemoaning his misfortune, he resolved to work harder than ever to do those things that mattered most to him before he died. In the following years he wrote many books and achieved a great deal. At the age of 92 he was still writing, having long since outrun his supposed terminal condition. He was definitely not lazy, and he became very wealthy as a result of all the work he did.

There is no doubt that the Scripture for today is true—hard work and diligence do bring reward and wealth, especially when what you do is under the leadership of God's Holy Spirit, properly applied with wisdom. Laziness is something that is universally condemned throughout the Scriptures. Paul was very blunt in his letter to the Thessalonians when he said, "If a man will not work, he shall not eat" (2 Thessalonians 3:10). Through my years in business I learned the hard way that good ideas, even God ideas, will remain as such if you never put in the work to make them happen.

There are seasons of harvest in all of our lives, when things have built up to a point of fulfillment—and that is definitely not a season to take time off and rest. If the crop is not reaped, poverty will result. But it is also true that if the ground is not properly prepared and the seed is not sown, there will not be any harvest at all. In every stage of life there is work to do, because in every season there is a purpose to fulfill.

And this is just as true in terms of the spiritual work that we do for the Kingdom of God. I was part of the team that worked behind the scenes to prepare for the last major mission that Billy Graham led in the U.K. It was called Mission England. A great harvest of people gave their lives to the Lord at the series of events, which was the spiritual equivalent of a farmer's harvested crop. But people behind the scenes had been working incredibly hard preparing the ground for at least three years, making sure that every single detail was thought through in advance of the time of harvest. Lives were changed and transformed at harvesttime because the "farmers" had been doing their work.

There is no shortage of work we can do for the Kingdom of God—let us do it with all our hearts knowing that the size and the quality of the harvest depends on the bit we do.

Thank You, Lord, for the warnings of Scripture not to be lazy. Forgive me, Lord, for times in my life when I have been deliberately lazy. Help me to be wise at every stage of my life and to learn Your wisdom about the things You want me to do—and then to do them with all my heart. In Jesus' name, Amen.

DAY 7

Day 8

FALSE ACCUSATIONS

Do not accuse a man for no reason—when he has done you no harm.

Proverbs 3:30

Telling lies in order to accuse a person falsely is a heinous crime. Damaging the reputation of someone is an act of robbery of far greater significance than stealing his goods—you are stealing his good name. Goods can be replaced, but when mud has been thrown at someone by telling lies about him or her for some ulterior motive, the sad fact is that some of that mud will stick in the minds of those who hear. They will think that there must be at least a grain of truth in what is being said, even if there is not.

Jesus suffered greatly from such false accusations. The words of the Pharisees, who concocted false stories about Him, would eventually be used to drive the nails through His hands and His feet when He was crucified. Yes, ruining someone's reputation by false accusation is a serious sin—it is like an act of murder.

We need to be very careful, therefore, when talking about others disrespectfully. We need to be especially careful about pointing the finger at others when we are trying to cover up secret sin in our own lives. Jesus hated and condemned such hypocrisy. At one time I was publicly accused, in the most abusive and degrading sort of way, by the minister of a large church. He declared that I was "in deception" because I was bringing healing and deliverance to Christians. I could not understand why this man, whom I had never met, was so keen to destroy me and my reputation. But a few years later it was discovered that he had had a secret ungodly relationship for many years. His fear of being exposed had driven him to attack any ministry that might, with discernment, see what was happening in his own life!

The Pharisees brought to Jesus a woman who had been caught in an act of adultery (see John 8:3–11). They wanted to see if He would be true to the Law of Moses and affirm that she should be stoned to death. But in response, Jesus challenged the hearts of her accusers and said something like, "Okay, but only throw a stone if you are without sin." Jesus knew what was in their hearts and that they had deliberately brought this woman to Jesus in order to try to trap Him. Their motives were evil.

If you have been falsely accused in a public place, you know the pain that lying words can cause. There is only one remedy for the pain within— forgiveness and God's inner comfort. Yes, the individual might not deserve to be forgiven—but Jesus died for our sins, and we do not deserve to be forgiven either! To speak out forgiveness toward those who have accused us falsely is like cutting the ropes that have tied those false accusations to our hearts.

And if we have been guilty of hypocritically speaking negatively about other people, for whatever reason—and especially when the things we are saying could just as easily be said of us—then it is time for personal repentance, asking God for forgiveness and a change of heart.

I am sorry, Lord, for the times when I have said wrong things about other people, for whatever reason. Please forgive me. And help me, Lord, to speak out my forgiveness of those who have hurt me with their false words. In Jesus' name, Amen.

DAY 8

Day 9

HOW WISE ARE YOU?

"Do not rebuke a mocker or he will hate you; rebuke a wise man and he will love you. Instruct a wise man and he will be wiser still; teach a righteous man and he will add to his learning."

Proverbs 9:8–9

It is never easy to receive correction, especially when you believe that you are right! But Proverbs 9 warns us that how we receive correction can be an indicator of how wise we are. Every time that we are corrected is an opportunity to learn and become wiser still.

I soon learned as a teenager that there were things I had gotten wrong—and that if I chose not to receive the correction gladly, I would be on a very slippery downhill slope. Soon there would be a price to pay. But I never liked receiving correction, for it showed off my ignorance. My pride had been dented!

Without correction, I would never have learned some of life's most important lessons. Students would never grow wiser if their teachers marked their schoolwork as if it were right, when it was wrong. Receiving correction is a vital part of the learning and growing process. And in the school of life, we never cease to be students.

But when it comes to correcting others in adult life, we first need to be very discerning of their heart attitudes. Today's Scripture reminds us that if the heart of someone is filled with mockery, he will not only refuse to receive correction but will actually hate you. And hatred is a murderous weapon that lies at the root of much evil intent. You cannot reason with someone who is motivated by hatred and, sadly, he or she usually has to learn life's lessons the hard way. Wisdom says that sometimes we have to wait until people are ready to listen before it is possible to bring any correction into their lives.

So, how do you react when you sense the Lord wants to confront and correct you? Are you ready to listen? Do you welcome His invitation when He says, as in the words of Isaiah 1:18, "'Come now, let us reason together,' says the LORD. 'Though your sins are like scarlet, they shall be as white as snow; though they are red as crimson, they shall be like wool.'"

The prophet Nathan had to confront David about his sin of adultery with Bathsheba and the murder of her husband, Uriah (see 2 Samuel 12). David had two choices: Do I humble myself, own up and repent? Or do I rebel and kill God's prophet? He made the right choice. Nothing could undo what he had done, but the way was now open for God to forgive and restore him. Psalm 51 is David's expression of his confession and repentance.

So how would you have responded if you had been in David's shoes? Would you have resisted the loving entreaties of the Lord when your behavior was so dramatically challenged? In verse 19 of chapter 1, Isaiah goes on to say, "If you are willing and obedient, you will eat the best from the land." But he warns us of serious consequences if we rebel against God (see verse 20).

A wise man will listen to the Lord and choose to walk in His ways. Even though David had sinned grievously, he was, nevertheless, a wise man and through this experience learned lessons that he would never forget.

Thank You, Lord, for both the challenge and the encouragement of Your Word. Forgive me, Lord, for those times when I have responded badly to necessary correction. Help me to receive Your correction gladly when You see me going off course, so that I will grow wiser and know more of Your blessing. In Jesus' name, Amen.

DAY 9

Day 10

PURE OR POLLUTED?

*Like a muddied spring or a polluted well is a righteous man who gives
way to the wicked.*

Proverbs 25:26

Springs and wells are sources of pure water—water that quenches the
thirst, satisfies the taste and is life-giving to all who drink it. But if that
life-giving water has become polluted or muddied, then it is undrinkable.
It is no longer life-giving and could even be life-threatening. When a river
becomes polluted with, for example, industrial effluent, the fish in the river
die. All the water is still there; it is what has been added to the water that
causes the problem.

   In just the same way, someone could have lived a righteous life and been
known as a true believer, but if the stream of truth that comes from his
mouth, or is evident in his life, has become polluted with deceptive beliefs,

practices or ungodly living, then his life has become poison to those who "drink" from that stream. They will be influenced by the pollutants and led astray into the same or similar sins. It takes only a small amount of poison in water to do a massive amount of damage. In just the same way, it takes only a small amount of deception in our lives to have the potential for leading many people astray.

A minister came to ask me once why I thought it was that so many people in his congregation were getting caught in sexual sin, in spite of being in a church where the Word of God was clearly preached. When I asked about the history of his church's leadership, he told me that a previous minister was found to be in an affair with a member of the choir. He was asked to leave, and the whole affair was covered up by the leaders because they did not want to bring the church into disrepute. When a leader sins in this way, a spirit is released into the fellowship and given license to influence his hearers. I was not surprised at the outcome. The spiritual air had become polluted, and people were breathing in deception.

No wonder Paul was so urgent in teaching his young disciple Timothy. He told him: "Watch your life and doctrine closely. Persevere in them, because if you do, you will save both yourself and your hearers" (1 Timothy 4:16). The implication is that if we allow pollutants in, they will affect our beliefs and our way of life. The damage could be fatal—to us individually, and to all those who listen to the music of our lives and are tempted to follow our example.

The fact that we may have years of godly living behind us does not mean that we are incapable of being led astray. The enemy will work extra hard to pollute the life streams of those who are in a position to influence others. How important it is that we guard our hearts and are very careful about where we put down our feet on the road of life—only going where the Lord is leading and only doing those things that please Him!

Thank You, Lord, for the warnings that You have placed in Your Word. Thank You that You have put them there to help us stay on the right path throughout our days. I pray that You will cleanse me from my sins, Lord, and help me to keep the water of my life free from pollutants, so that it will always be fresh and life-giving to all with whom I relate or have influence. In Jesus' name, Amen.

DAY 10

Day 11

SETTING A TRUE COURSE

He holds victory in store for the upright, he is a shield to those whose walk is blameless, for he guards the course of the just and protects the way of his faithful ones.

Proverbs 2:7–8

Some years ago, I devoted a year of my life to writing material for an online daily training school, which is now published in book form as the Journey to Freedom series (Chosen, 2019). My heart's desire was to help people know how to walk in the ways of God and be able to set a true course for their lives. If we truly walk on the path that He has laid out for us, then there are many, many promises in Scripture pointing out the blessings God has in store for His children.

The many blessings that God promises in His Word are an outworking of His covenant love for His children. This one passage alone promises victory (in the battles of life) to those who are upright—those who deliberately make godly choices when facing temptation.

Then, if our walk is blameless, we are promised a shield of protection. What does that mean? I believe it simply means that when our heart's desire is for God's Kingdom authority to be established in our lives, then the angels of God will rejoice to be there for us—just as they were for Jesus in His wilderness experience of being tested by the devil. We will never know till we reach eternity just how often we have unknowingly experienced God's protection and deliverance.

One day, as I was driving my car, I had to turn to the left up a long gentle hill. As I put my foot down and accelerated, the driver's door of my car suddenly flung open! Immediately I took my foot off the gas, applied the brake, slowed right down and stretched out my hand to close the door. Then, as I looked up again at the road ahead, a young child on a tricycle came hurtling down a sloping driveway and went straight out onto the road where I would have been had the door not mysteriously flung open at that critical moment. I have no doubt that God saved that child's life and saved me from the terrible trauma of having killed a child.

When setting sail for a long voyage, the most important thing we need to know is how to navigate. If we cannot set a true course, we will be lost at sea forever. When we set out to be just and fair in all we think, say and do, God promises us His wisdom as we plot the course of our lives—not just in the overall big picture of where we are going, but also in the microdetails of today's part of the journey. He is a faithful God.

What tremendous blessings come from our walking in the ways of the Lord; Psalm 19:7 expresses the blessings in terms of revival! All over the world many of God's people are crying out to Him for revival. But God's Word tells us that we can have personal revival wherever we are—all that God looks for is the heart that is turned toward Him and a will that has chosen to respond in obedience to His love.

Thank You, Lord, for the many times Your hand of protection and direction has been operating in my life. Help me always to have such a heart for You and Your ways that I will consistently choose to follow You in all the activities and details of my life, knowing that You will guide and direct my steps. In Jesus' name, Amen.

DAY 11

Day 12

RESIST ENTICEMENT

My son, if sinners entice you, do not give in to them. . . . Do not go along with them, do not set foot on their paths; for their feet rush into sin.

Proverbs 1:10, 15–16

The word *entice* means "to tempt or to lead astray." It carries with it all the connotations of exciting, but ungodly, activities—things that fascinate the carnal nature and that, if we are honest, all of us can be vulnerable to from time to time. Everything from greed to lust, and a whole lot of desires between these two extremes, can get stirred up when enticement is in the air.

In these very testing days, when many people are struggling to hold things together financially and moral boundaries are disintegrating like snow in the sun, many are fighting a sense of hopelessness, even despair. At times like this, enticement is especially dangerous. People look for some form of comfort or escape from the pressures they are enduring and are that much more vulnerable to temptations when they come—whether they come in the form of making money, having a wrong relationship or simply indulging in selfish and unproductive activity.

When times are tough, whether that season is totally personal to you or part of a national or international situation, the enemy will always try to take advantage of what is going on, to entice you into something ungodly. He tries to stand in the place of God and be a source of comfort, not telling his victims that his sort of comfort will always prove to be false.

Paul was very explicit about the only source of true comfort when he said,

> Praise be to the God and Father of our Lord Jesus Christ, the Father of compassion and the God of all comfort, who comforts us in all our troubles, so that we can comfort those in any trouble with the comfort we ourselves have received from God.

> 2 Corinthians 1:3–4

Herein lies a model for each one of our lives. Once we have learned how to receive true relational comfort from Father God for ourselves, without seeking the enticements of the enemy, we are then equipped to be able to give the same unconditional loving comfort to others, who may not yet have learned how to draw on the Father's love for their own inner comfort. In so doing we become the hands and heart of God to them and a means of preventing people from seeking the enticements of the enemy and being led astray because of their unmet needs.

When John penned the letters from Jesus to the seven churches, recorded in Revelation 2 and 3, each one highlighted issues and problems that needed to be dealt with in the churches, but then ended with strong words to endure and overcome. Jesus was encouraging them so that, in testing times, the enemy would not rob them of their inheritance.

I urge you not to let anyone be used by the enemy to entice you to sample the pleasures of what John Bunyan called "Vanity Fair" in his amazing book *Pilgrim's Progress*. Vanity Fair displays all the enticements of the enemy and is designed by Satan to rob you of your inheritance in God. Each of us must learn to ignore all such enticements and press on, running the race of life till that day when the gates of heaven open at the end of the journey!

I am sorry, Lord, for those times when I have sought false comfort through the enemy's enticements. Help me, Lord, to recognize enticements of the enemy when they come and then to endure and overcome whatever obstacles stand in the way of my destiny in God. In Jesus' name, Amen.

DAY 12

Day 13

HONESTY *IS* THE BEST POLICY

Kings detest wrongdoing, for a throne is established through righteousness. Kings take pleasure in honest lips; they value a man who speaks the truth.

Proverbs 16:12–13

Some time ago there were the most extraordinary scenes in the British Houses of Parliament. Members of Parliament (MPs) were suddenly rushing to pay back money to the government that they should never have taken!

All MPs are rightfully entitled to make claims for necessary expenses in doing their jobs, but for years a culture of dishonesty had ruled in the seat of government. Many MPs, of all political parties, were caught red-handed claiming money by way of expenses that had nothing whatsoever to do with their jobs. And the nation was rightfully outraged.

These people, who were responsible for putting laws into place that other people have to obey, had been systematically and dishonestly milking the system for their own benefit. But when they were all exposed (by an investigative journalist on a national newspaper), they began desperately trying to pay the money back, thinking that if they paid it back quickly, they could get away with keeping their reputations. Never before had I seen such a display of public hypocrisy!

I fear for any nation when there is unrighteousness at its core. As our Scripture for today says, thrones (governments) are established through righteousness. The converse of this is that governments are destroyed by unrighteousness.

The stories of the kings of Israel and Judah contain many illustrations of what can happen when governments get it wrong. Read how Jehoshaphat, for example, wrongfully entered into a business relationship to build a fleet of ships with evil King Ahaziah (see 2 Chronicles 20:35–37). He lost God's protection, and the whole of the fleet was destroyed.

But before we come down with a heavy hand of judgment upon those in public office who have acted without integrity (not all MPs were implicated; many had acted in total honesty and not claimed any money falsely), let us examine our own hearts.

Is it not possible that there could be things in our own lives (things we think about, say or do) that are dishonest and, therefore, ungodly? And I wonder how we would be behaving now if an angelic journalist on a Kingdom newspaper were to expose these things publicly for everyone else to know about? My guess is that we might be moving very quickly to try to put things right!

One day, at the end of time, everything that is unconfessed and unfor-given will be exposed for all to see. So, perhaps we should learn from this sad episode in British parliamentary history and seek to put things right in our lives now, and not wait for the public exposure that will otherwise come to all in eternity. In that way our lives, our families, our churches, our cities and even our nations can be established in righteousness—and be strong.

Lord, I am sorry for the deceptions operating in both my nation and my own private life. I ask that You forgive me for all the dishonest hidden things that have operated in my life, and help me to put things right. Thank You that Your Word shows us clearly what is right and what is wrong. In Jesus' name, Amen.

DAY 13

Day 14

AN UNDEFENDABLE CITY

Like a city whose walls are broken down is a man who lacks self-control.

Proverbs 25:28

A while ago my wife and I visited Hadrian's Wall—that huge stone wall that crosses from the west to the east along northern England. It was built by the Romans to protect this furthermost border of the Roman Empire from the wild and dangerous Scots, who lived in the hill country beyond the wall. As I looked at this amazing structure, much of which still stands strong and wide today, after nearly two thousand years, I imagined how difficult it would be for invaders to cross the wall in the face of the constant patrols of Roman soldiers, who paraded up and down the top of the wall, 24 hours a day.

Many ancient cities in the world were surrounded by high strong walls as a defense against invading armies. It was news of the broken-down walls of Jerusalem (see Nehemiah 1:3) that moved Nehemiah's heart, as he prayed for his home city and his people. Hearing that the walls were still broken down and the gates burnt brought him to grief. He knew God was calling him to do something about it. Nehemiah's book covers the whole story from beginning to end, of how God used him to take on and complete the task and restore the safety of the city. Without complete walls, the city was defenseless.

Today's Scripture likens the broken-down walls of a person's life to the broken-down walls of a city. Control of our conduct and behavior is a vital protection against the invasion of the enemy into our lives. Paul explained carefully in Galatians 6:7–8 how there are consequences for living a life that is not self-controlled and in godly order. The fact is, just as a city with broken-down walls is undefendable, so is a person's life that is out of control.

Without the Holy Spirit, none of us will have the strength to resist the attacks of the enemy. We all need that spirit of self-control that the Lord will give us if we ask Him. The problem is that many people enjoy too much the things that come in through the gap in our defenses, and the Lord cannot help us win a battle that we actually want to lose.

A woman asked for prayer. There were issues in her life that seemed impossible for her to overcome. But during a teaching I gave at a conference, she had been convicted about an area in her life where her personal walls were well and truly broken down. As office manager of the company where she worked, she was responsible for handling all the petty cash. In her heart she believed she was worth more to the company than she actually got paid. So, for many years she had systematically fiddled the books and paid herself extra out of petty cash.

The teaching from God's words brought conviction into her heart. She realized that over the years she had stolen many thousands of dollars from the people who trusted her to handle the petty cash with integrity. It was not surprising, therefore, that God could not answer her prayers while there was such a glaring hole in the walls of her life. The key to her healing came when, in tears of deep repentance, she started to put matters right—both with God and with her employers.

There are many possible reasons why the walls of our personal cities could be broken down due to lack of self-control. Let's pray that God will give each of us the desire for all the gaps in our defenses to be filled in and then ask Him to show us how to do it. Then our lives will be strong and effective for Him—and what is more, we will be more blessed than we ever dreamed possible!

Help me, Lord, to identify those areas of my life where there are gaps in the defenses of my soul. I choose now to want to have defendable walls, so that the enemy will no longer have access to the center of my life. In Jesus' name, Amen.

DAY 14

THE HIGHWAY CODE FOR GOD

Where there is no revelation, the people cast off restraint; but blessed is he who keeps the law.

Proverbs 29:18

The Highway Code is a document that sets out in detail and with great clarity exactly what drivers in the U.K. can and cannot do on British roads. It is an important publication that is at the heart of all road safety. If people do not know or understand the Highway Code, then they will, inevitably, make mistakes. When drivers ignore these wise legal restraints, then accidents, injuries and even death could be the result.

Without wise restraints there is always danger. This is true in many areas of life. At one point there was much heavy rain in the U.K.; some areas of the country were subject to severe flooding. People died when the floodwaters broke the banks of a river and the formerly placid stream became a raging torrent, sweeping away everything in its path.

A river is a wonderful blessing when it is contained within the restraint of its banks, but once the restraint has been breached the water goes everywhere; people's homes are flooded and there is danger. Strong restraints make the river safe.

The laws of God are meant to act like the Highway Code and the banks of a river, restraining our behavior so that we never venture into dangerous territory. But when we lose appreciation for the fact that God's laws are designed by Him to keep us safe, then it is easy for us to succumb to the temptations that take us beyond those barriers of safety.

As I write this devotional, the newspapers are full of news of the tragic death of one of Britain's richest women—she had everything she could possibly have wanted. Her house was said to have been worth seventy million pounds. But she and her husband had lived a life without restraint, addicted to drugs. Her life ended at a tragically early age. If only she had learned to live her life according to the revelation of truth in the Word of God.

When we choose to respect God's Word truly as revelation from God Himself and begin to respect the restraints that God in His love and wisdom provided for us, we lay down a foundation of blessing—not only for our own lives, but also for the lives of our children and grandchildren. When we gladly live within those restraints, we find ourselves constantly discovering the many blessings God wants us to enjoy.

Because we have free will, however, people find it tempting to laugh at those restraints and choose to live life their own way. They will eventually discover that there is a law of sowing and reaping—and it is only good seed that produces a good crop. If you need convincing about the blessings that come to those who keep God's laws, then spend a quiet hour reading Psalm 119. Just as the Highway Code is the blueprint for safe driving, Psalm 119 is the Highway Code for God-blessed living.

Thank You, Lord, that You love us enough to show us how restraints can be a source of blessing in our lives. Help me, Lord, to welcome the application of Your laws in my life. In Jesus' name, Amen.

DAY 15

Day 16

THE LAMP OF GOD

The lamp of the Lord searches the spirit of a man; it searches out his
innermost being.

Proverbs 20:27

Our eyesight can change over the years. Recently I needed a new pair of glasses. In one part of the eye exam, the optician used a brilliant pinpoint of light to look through the lens of my eye and examine the condition of my retina. Her lamp was searching out the innermost recesses of my eyes. I was relieved when she reported that everything was in good order.

In a similar way, the Holy Spirit is the lamp of God who reaches beyond the exterior of our lives to test our spirits and search out the recesses of our innermost being—those places where we can even try to hide things from ourselves. The places where the thoughts and the intentions of our hearts can reside and act as motivators of the soul.

As a consequence of his extraordinary and life-changing encounter with almighty God, the young Isaiah was forced to look at himself afresh. In the face of the blinding light of revelation that came into him as a result of seeing the glory of God, he became acutely aware of his own inner uncleanness. He was totally undone by the experience (see Isaiah 6:1–5). Hebrews 4:13 tells us that nothing is hidden from God's sight. The thoughts and the intentions of our hearts are open to His view.

Our innermost being is the source of the decisions we make and the things we do—both good and bad. It is here that the motives of the heart have their origin, and Proverbs 16:2 tells us that it is the motives that are weighed by the Lord.

It is easy for us to deceive ourselves and for our ways to seem innocent to us (as it also says in Proverbs 16:2), even though they may be far from innocent. As a result, we become blinded, even to what those innermost motives are. We need help—and help is at hand, for this Scripture tells us that the lamp of the Lord will search out our innermost being. But we need to give Him permission to show us the truth about ourselves.

So often we pray with people who need help with a seemingly obvious problem—but it is not the real issue. A pastor once told me I had saved the life of one of his church members. She weighed 350 pounds and was eating herself to death. No amount of self-discipline or prayer seemed to help.

As she and I talked and asked the Lord to shine His lamp on her life, she was reminded of the day when her husband left her by sticking a note on her refrigerator door to say that he had left her for someone else. On that day she opened the fridge door and began to comfort herself with what was inside. Twenty years later she was still doing it. When God opened her heart to forgive and receive His healing, her desire to comfort herself with food disappeared, and she lost weight rapidly. Her life was indeed saved through the penetrating light of the Holy Spirit—the lamp of God.

So, our prayer today is simply to ask the Lord to shine His lamp into the recesses of our hearts and to show us what He sees. We then need to take time to listen to the Lord and to welcome His presence. It is at times like these that the Lord has not only shown me things that I need to address in my life but also has whispered things into my heart that have subsequently become of great significance in the direction my life should take.

Thank You, Lord, that You are able to see into the inner recesses of my heart. Please shine Your lamp and help me to see those things that are displeasing to You, so that, with Your help, I can make lasting and fruitful changes in my life. And then envision me afresh so that the motives of my heart will always be to please You. In Jesus' name, Amen.

DAY 16

Day 17

RICH OR POOR?

"Keep falsehood and lies far from me; give me neither poverty nor riches, but give me only my daily bread. Otherwise, I may have too much and disown you and say, 'Who is the Lord?' Or I may become poor and steal, and so dishonor the name of my God."

Proverbs 30:8–9

We all like having money to spend, so it takes an unusual degree of spiritual wisdom to pray this prayer—a prayer that is designed to help us maintain godly stability, with appropriate income for the lives God has called us to live.

This Scripture highlights the dangers that can lie at the opposite ends of this scale. If we have too little we may, in desperation, be tempted to use ungodly ways such as dishonesty, cheating or stealing to try to fix things for ourselves. But if we have too much, then the riches could take the focus of our eyes off the pathways of life that the Lord wants us to follow. It is possible to remain faithful to God, even if facing poverty or gaining great wealth, but both are potentially dangerous.

Benjamin Franklin once commented on this dilemma by saying: "Contentment makes poor men rich; discontent makes rich men poor." He was taking his cue from Paul's words to his trainee evangelist, Timothy:

> Godliness with contentment is great gain. For we brought nothing into the world, and we can take nothing out of it. But if we have food and clothing, we will be content with that. People who want to get rich fall into temptation and a trap and into many foolish and harmful desires that plunge [people] into ruin and destruction. For the love of money is a root of all kinds of evil. Some people, eager for money, have wandered from the faith and pierced themselves with many griefs.
>
> 1 Timothy 6:6–10

Paul's early life had been immersed, as a Pharisee, in the study of the Scriptures, and today's verse would have been very familiar to him. No doubt, he had seen the reality of both ends of the spectrum—how poverty and hunger can become an ungodly driving force in a person's life, and how wealth and the discontent with what one has creates the desire for more and more wealth. That also becomes an insatiable driving force.

There is a further problem with wealth, because the fact that people can buy whatever they want with their money makes their riches an idol—one that is worshiped every single day. When God answered Solomon's prayer for wisdom, the young man was given the ability to know and speak out God's truth. But in the fleshly areas of his life, he ceased to listen to the

Holy Spirit's voice of wisdom and was led astray by the women in his life, even building temples for them to worship their pagan gods.

If only Solomon had listened to his own teaching, it would have saved him from many troubles. Many times people have made *If only . . .* statements to me—especially relating to how they spent their lives. They never learned to be content with living a godly life, and then twenty or thirty years later, they were forced by circumstances to face the consequences of the choices they had made.

Perhaps it is time in your life to learn to be content with God whatever your physical circumstances—to trust Him to be your provider when you are in need and ask Him for wisdom and courage as to how to use the wealth that you have.

Thank You, Lord, for Your faithfulness. Forgive me, Lord, for times when, out of need, I have been tempted to do wrong things. And forgive me for times when my desire for more wealth has unleashed a spirit of greed that has driven me away from You. Help me, Lord, to be content in You—knowing that godly contentment is treasure beyond understanding. In Jesus' name, Amen.

DAY 17

Day 18

WHEN I WAS A BOY

When I was a boy in my father's house, still tender, and an only child of my mother, he taught me and said, "Lay hold of my words with all your heart; keep my commands and you will live. Get wisdom, get understanding; do not forget my words or swerve from them."

Proverbs 4:3–5

How I thank God that at the age of nine I knelt at my bedside with my father and invited Jesus into my heart! I have never forgotten that most important moment in the whole of my life. I will never cease to be thankful for a dad (and a mum) who saw it as their loving duty to teach me the ways of the Lord when I was young—before I reached the impressionable teenage years, when it is so easy for young people to go astray and, as they say, do their own thing.

Doing one's own thing can be extremely risky, for having the developing physique and unbridled will of a young person without the maturity of an adult can lead to big mistakes of lifelong consequence.

When we learn to respect our elders, we will listen to what they have to say. And the wisdom that comes from their maturity becomes the wisdom that helps young people negotiate the traps that the enemy never ceases to lay in their paths. We live, however, in a generation in which respect for the wisdom of our elders has been replaced with information acquired at the click of a mouse or via a mobile phone. And information, without the maturity and wisdom as to how it should be used, will always be a massive trap for young people.

Such information will never trump the spiritual wisdom the writer of Proverbs is referring to. For this is the wisdom from the heart of God, which God intended to be passed on from generation to generation.

As I thought about this, I was overwhelmed by a sense of responsibility that parents, grandparents, great-grandparents, uncles and aunts have to pray for the children in the family and to lead them gently to faith in Jesus when they are young. Then, imparting the wisdom of their years to the upcoming generations gives them a chance to navigate the pitfalls of life. With the wisdom of the older generations to aid them on their journeys, they will be much better equipped to enter into their destinies in God. And who knows what blessings there will be down the years as a result!

Even when we have not personally had the blessing of a human father or mother who taught us God's wisdom when we were young, our heavenly Father has ensured that we can still be led and directed by His wisdom, through the written Word of God. The world may not respect the precious truths the Bible contains, but we do not have to follow the ways of the world. God has given us free will, and when we use it to make godly choices and not swerve off the Royal Highway laid out for us by the King of kings, then we can be sure that the promises of God will be as true for us as if we had been taught them from an early age.

Thank You, Lord, for all those who have imparted the wisdom of God into my life. Help me to exercise my own spiritual responsibility by imparting Your wisdom to the children and young people who are part of my wider family. In Jesus' name, Amen.

Day 19

THE CURRENCY OF HEAVEN

Wealth is worthless in the day of wrath, but righteousness delivers from death. The righteousness of the blameless makes a straight way for them, but the wicked are brought down by their own wickedness.

Proverbs 11:4–5

Wealth and riches can be used to bring enormous blessing to many people, if they are used wisely and generously in the Lord's service. We may spend all our lives trying to accumulate large amounts of money—but the fact is, we can only use our physical resources while we are here on earth. Nothing of what we physically own on our earthly pilgrimage will carry any weight or give us any influence when we finally have to face God. We cannot take any of it with us. All our money and human resources will count for nothing on the day that Solomon described here as being "the day of wrath."

The power and influence that wealth can exercise on earth is reduced to nothing when we stand before God. Earthly gold, silver and treasure are not the currency of heaven. The currency of heaven is the "righteousness of the blameless." Jesus told a parable to help people understand how important it is to be ready, having a good supply of the sort of currency that does carry weight in eternity.

In the parable (see Matthew 25), ten young women were waiting for the bridegroom to come. Five had a good supply of oil for their lamps; the others had none. When it became clear that the bridegroom was finally coming, panic set in among the five without oil with which to light their lamps, so they went off to try to find some—but it was too late. The bridegroom came, and they missed their opportunity. Only those who already had oil for their lamps could go with Him.

Jesus is, of course, the Bridegroom, and the Body of Christ is the Bride. Only those who have truly humbled themselves at the foot of the cross and received Jesus as their Savior and Lord are capable of being made righteous and are able to be part of the Bride. And when the fruit of our lives is assessed, it is only that which has been done in obedient response to His love that will carry weight when the books are finally opened at the end of time (see Revelation 20:11–12).

This is the currency of heaven, the righteousness that "delivers from death" and that makes a way straight ahead of us in the journey of life. It is vitally important that our trust for daily living is not in whatever resources we may or may not have, but in the God who loved us so much that He sent that which was most precious to Him, His Son, to express His love toward us.

When we trust in Him and follow Him in joyful obedience, we are storing up for ourselves eternal wealth that can be measured only in the currency of heaven. While God can use money to facilitate His Kingdom purposes here on earth, let's not fall into the trap of trusting in what we have now, thinking that this will give us credibility in heaven.

It won't.

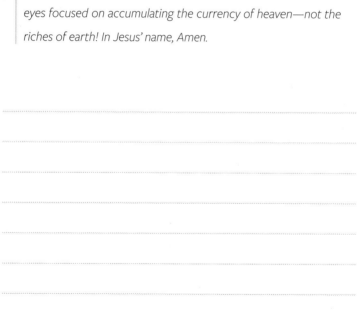

Thank You, Lord, for the blessings I can bestow on others through the resources You have given me to do my share in building the Kingdom of God. I ask that You will forgive me, Lord, for ever thinking that any earthly wealth will give me status before You. Help me to be wise with the resources You have given me and to keep my eyes focused on accumulating the currency of heaven—not the riches of earth! In Jesus' name, Amen.

DAY 19

Day 20

DEAF EARS

If anyone turns a deaf ear to the law, even his prayers are detestable.
He who leads the upright along an evil path will fall into his own trap,
but the blameless will receive a good inheritance.

Proverbs 28:9–10

When someone is said to "turn a deaf ear," that does not mean the person is physically incapable of hearing. It simply means he or she is choosing to ignore what is being said. God's Word very clearly expresses both God's heart of love for mankind and the way He wants us to live. The Ten Commandments are referred to in Deuteronomy 4:13 as God's covenant. God's covenant is an expression of His loving provision for His people. There can be no confusion over what His Word says—especially in the fundamental areas of morality.

When faced with temptation, people have to make choices in many areas of their lives. Most believers know that choosing to walk in God's paths is the way to enjoy His blessings—for, as the second part of our Scripture says, "the blameless will receive a good inheritance." Most believers also know that sin has consequences as well. But few people realize that in addition to the direct consequences of sin—sin is rebellion against God—there is a serious secondary consequence of deliberately turning a deaf ear to what God says in His Word: Our prayers are no longer acceptable to Him.

This truth was also spoken out by the prophet Isaiah, at a time when God's people were in serious rebellion against Him. God said, "When you spread out your hands in prayer, I will hide my eyes from you; even if you offer many prayers, I will not listen" (Isaiah 1:15). When we turn a deaf ear toward God's Word and choose deliberately to flout His laws, then God responds in like manner: He no longer listens to our prayers. This is a principle that applies to individuals, organizations, congregations and even nations, as the people of Israel found out to their detriment on numerous occasions.

Often people ask, "Why doesn't God answer my prayers?" While there may be many different answers to this question, the one answer we do not want to hear could be that God is turning a deaf ear toward us because of our deliberate sin! When our behavior tells God that we do not really care about Him, then it is not surprising that our prayers become an offense to Him. It is not that God has no love for us and is not interested in our prayers; it is simply that our actions toward Him are speaking louder than the words we might say to Him.

If we want to regain a place of authority in prayer, so that we will know about and experience the power of prayer at work in our lives, then let's determine that the actions of our lives and the words of our lips be truly in harmony with each other. When they are, God has no problem hearing and answering our prayers. But when our actions are speaking a different language from our lips, then we are in great danger.

Thank You, Lord, for showing me that there can be a relationship between what I do and whether or not You hear and answer my prayers. Forgive me, Lord, for the times when I have deliberately chosen to sin even while thinking You should be answering my prayers. Help me, Lord, to live my whole life in harmony with Your Word so that I can be a person of spiritual integrity and know the blessing of answered prayer. In Jesus' name, Amen.

DAY 20

Day 21

A MATTER OF LIFE AND DEATH

Whoever gives heed to instruction prospers, and blessed is he who trusts in the Lord. . . . There is a way that seems right to a man, but in the end it leads to death.

Proverbs 16:20, 25

It is not wrong to want to prosper—there are many verses in the Bible that promise prosperity—but the general understanding of what the word *prosperity* means is significantly different from what the Bible teaches!

As is clear from this verse, one of the keys to becoming prosperous in God's way is not only to listen to the instruction that comes right to our spirits from Him and the Word of God, but also to heed that instruction. This means apply the teaching to our lives and keep walking forward in obedience.

In the years before the work of Ellel Ministries started, I was a publisher, running my own companies. I desperately wanted them to be successful. One day a book proposal came to me through which I thought I could make a lot of money—and become prosperous. The only problem was that God spoke to my heart and told me not to have anything to do with the man who was writing that book.

Because I wanted to be prosperous in my own way, I deliberately closed my heart to the instruction of the Lord, thinking that I knew better than God. That was the biggest mistake I ever made in my business career. It very nearly cost me everything I had; at one stage I was hovering between bankruptcy and being murdered!

I was deeply repentant for what I had done and cried out to God for Him to save and deliver me, for the man was threatening to take my very life. God heard my prayer and amazingly delivered me. But I very nearly discovered the hard way the most severe meaning of the second part of this verse: "There is a way that seems right to a man, but in the end it leads to death."

Through that experience, I learned the most important lesson of my life—that God's instructions matter, and that when He speaks it is not a good idea to disobey His voice. On other occasions, when I did obey the Lord and allowed Him to direct my steps and the way I ran the business, I had some remarkable and blessed experiences, which led to prosperous outcomes.

And so, the message from this Scripture is simply to trust God and His Word and to listen for His instruction every day. It could be a matter of life and death. God has promised to show you the way to go, so that you can enjoy the blessing of His presence with you as you choose to resist the temptations of the evil one and walk in God's ways.

Thank You, Lord, that You have given us vital keys in Your Word to help us live for You and to enjoy the sort of prosperity You have planned for us. Forgive me, Lord, for the times when I have chosen to ignore Your gentle voice of instruction. Help me always to have the courage to obey You and Your Word. In the name of Jesus, Amen.

DAY 21

Day 22

GOD'S WAY OF WISDOM

A fool finds no pleasure in understanding but delights in airing his own opinions. . . . He who gets wisdom loves his own soul; he who cherishes understanding prospers.

Proverbs 18:2; 19:8

No one likes being called a fool, but sadly, many people behave foolishly regarding the things of God. Pride and arrogance reign in their lives—they think they know best and can do without any input from the God whom modern science has consigned to the trash can of religious history as an unnecessary myth. For them, the world invented itself and humankind is master of the universe.

But not having a knowledge or understanding of God's Word puts them in the situation of being ignorant about the most important things of life. The psalmist tells us that someone who says there is no God is a fool (see

Psalm 14:1). So, according to God's Word, even the cleverest scientist on the planet who denies the reality of God is, simply, a fool.

There are people, however, who believe that God exists but are still fools. They are so full of their own ideas that they never stop to consider whether or not those opinions are right or wrong. They rarely listen to what others are saying. As our Scripture today makes so very clear, they do not even seek to gain understanding. When God was speaking to His people through the prophet Hosea, He said, "My people are destroyed from lack of knowledge" (Hosea 4:6).

Faith is, of course, absolutely essential for salvation—for without faith it is impossible to please God (see Hebrews 11:6). But when it comes to our day-to-day living, as believers in God, we should be diligent to gain understanding—about God, the ways of God and the plans of God for us. With both faith and understanding, we will have a better perception on situations as they develop and be in a much better place to make good choices and godly decisions.

Many of the people whom I have had the privilege of ministering to over the years have had plenty of faith in God, but at times in their lives they made unwise decisions, failing to seek God's understanding and wisdom. And those choices sometimes left them with expensive lifetime consequences.

But the end of our Scripture for today encourages us with a wonderful promise—that if we cherish understanding and make godly choices, we will enjoy God's blessing on our lives. This is God's promise to His people.

The word *cherish* means "to love and care deeply for something or someone, to treasure, value highly and hold it dear within your heart." If we feel like that toward having knowledge and understanding about the things of God, then it will be for us as if the heart of God becomes ours. We will then understand things from His point of view. And there cannot be a better perspective for us to have on life!

Help me, Lord, always to seek to gain knowledge and understanding of You and Your ways, so that I will be in a much better position to make godly choices in all the future decisions of my life. In Jesus' name, Amen.

DAY 22

Day 23

UNWELCOME MESSAGES

He who listens to a life-giving rebuke will be at home among the wise. He who ignores discipline despises himself, but whoever heeds correction gains understanding. The fear of the Lord teaches a man wisdom, and humility comes before honor.

Proverbs 15:31–33

There are times in all our lives when we need to hear the truth about ourselves. But, frankly, none of us likes it. The natural instinct of our carnal nature is to rise up to attack the messenger instead of to listen carefully to the message, asking the Lord if there is any truth in what is being said. I can remember several times as a youth rising up on the inside and thinking my father was wrong in what he was saying. In later life, however, I realized just how right he was at the time and how important his loving correction had been. It saved me from making serious mistakes.

In the history of God's people there were many occasions when the prophets brought unwelcome messages. Instead of listening to what God was saying through His prophetic mouthpieces, they often turned on the prophets who had had the courage to tell the people the truth.

In Isaiah's day, for example, the people rebelled with these words: "Give us no more visions of what is right! Tell us pleasant things, prophesy illusions" (Isaiah 30:10). This is an extraordinary verse of Scripture. The people knew Isaiah to be a godly man who listened to the heart of God and always spoke the truth. But when they did not like hearing what he had to say, they asked this godly man to tell them lies. They did not want to hear the voice of God through Isaiah's corrective words. In pride and arrogance, they wanted to live life in their own ungodly ways. When someone speaks correction into our lives, let's not be hasty in rejecting the message.

Today's Scripture contains a salutary warning about the dangers of ignoring the voice of correction. It also gives us an interesting slant on the consequences of ignoring discipline. It says that he who ignores discipline despises himself! Discipline may not always be given in the best possible way, and it is rarely a comfortable experience. But when it comes, we need to weigh it carefully, for if we reject the message and choose to shoot the messenger instead, we are actually despising ourselves.

If you despise people, you look down on them and give them no respect. And if you despise yourself, that is exactly what you are doing. You are looking down on yourself and disrespecting the need there may be in your life to consider the message prayerfully and choose to change. The consequences could be serious, as they so often were for God's people when they rejected the messages of His prophets.

Our Scripture encourages us to listen carefully to the voice of correction, for it is through this that we can gain important understanding. But we will never be willing to walk that path unless first we deal with our pride and choose to humble ourselves. As that wonderful Bible teacher Derek Prince used to say, "The way down is the way up!"

I am sorry, Lord, for any times I have despised myself and not benefited from godly correction when it was given. Help me, Lord, to listen carefully when You bring correction into my life. Help me to welcome it so that I may gain understanding and more fully walk in Your ways. In Jesus' name, Amen.

Day 24

EIGHT WORDS THAT CAN SAVE YOUR LIFE

To fear the LORD is to hate evil.

Proverbs 8:13

I have recently been casting my mind back over the years of Ellel Ministries and thinking of all the stories I would want to put in a book about what God has done since the work began back in 1986. As I have done so, I have found myself also thinking about some of the people we would love to have helped more than we were able—people for whom the key to their situations lies within the eight words of our short Scripture for today.

These were people who said they really loved the Lord. People who had been touched by Him at different times in their lives, but people, nevertheless, who were still struggling with issues that seemed to overwhelm them at regular intervals. They found that the temptations of the world were too often greater than they felt they could handle, and they kept slipping back into a variety of sinful behaviors. Most often these were of a sexual nature. Some came back for ministry several times—each time deeply repentant. But at the core of their being something serious was out of order, which made them prone to temptation and sin.

When talking about healing, I often say that the best definition I know is this: the restoration of God's order in a person's life. This does not mean living life according to the way I would like things to be, but living according to the way God has said they should be. On this rock many people stumble. They want God to fit in with their ideas and desires—not the other way around! And at the end of the day, for some of these dear people, the real issue is not the size or the nature of their problems, but the simple fact that while they say they love the Lord, they have not yet learned to hate evil.

Many times, I have written or spoken about the simple relationship between *fear of the Lord* and *love for the Lord*. If you really love someone, you naturally do not want to do things that grieve that person. And so if you *really* love the Lord, the last thing you will ever want to do is to embrace any of the evil that separated mankind from God and that Jesus died on the cross to set us free from.

If you are struggling with temptation in any form today, let's not be afraid to ask the hard question: Have you fallen into the trap of loving this particular evil thing more than you love the Lord? If so, it may be time to repent—not so much of the sin associated with your problem, but of thinking it is okay not to hate evil, which is so often the real issue that underpins the problem of temptation. Loving evil will always separate us from God.

In the Lord's Prayer, Jesus encouraged us to pray *Deliver us from evil.* The fact is, however, that God cannot answer that prayer if we love evil more than we love Him.

Thank You, Lord, that You love people, such as me, so much that You sent Jesus to die for our sins, in spite of the evil that separated You from mankind. Help me, Lord, to recognize evil when I see it, before it becomes a temptation and a trap I can fall into. Help me, also, Lord, to hate evil and to choose to walk in the opposite direction when I am faced with ungodly choices. In Jesus' name, Amen.

DAY 24

Day 25

HOW DO YOU RECEIVE A REBUKE?

If you had responded to my rebuke, I would have poured out my heart
to you and made my thoughts known to you.

Proverbs 1:23

None of us likes to receive a rebuke. A rebuke given in love, however, is like the lines of a railway, keeping the engine and rail cars on track and going in the right direction. But there is an enemy within, which each one of us has to contend with, that hates a rebuke from the Lord. This enemy does everything it possibly can to rise up in rejection of the loving advice that is implicit within a rebuke from the Lord. And the name of that enemy? Pride!

When pride is given control of our emotions and our reactions, we put ourselves in a potentially dangerous place. And, what is more, we miss out on all that God is waiting to pour into our hearts in order to bless, encourage and direct our steps with His all-embracing love. He does not reject those He rebukes, for a rebuke from the Lord is a hallmark of His love (see Hebrews 12:6).

A rebuke from the Lord, correctly received, opens the doors of our souls to the leading of the Spirit of God and knowing God's thoughts for our lives. But if, as a result of our pride, we give God the signal that we do not want to hear His voice, He is not going to pour into our hearts all the things that He longs for us to understand.

In order to understand the ways of the Lord, we have to learn both to recognize His voice when He speaks and to respond gladly, even if what He says is a corrective rebuke. If we can learn to silence the voice of pride and listen instead to the leading of the Lord, He will be constantly speaking His wisdom into our hearts. Our lives will be kept safely on track.

This is exactly what Jesus had to do with Simon Peter. Peter had been given extraordinary revelation about who Jesus was: the Messiah, the Son of the living God (see Matthew 16:16). But then, only a short while later, when Jesus told the disciples that soon He would be killed and would rise again on the third day, Simon Peter rose up to challenge what Jesus had said. In so doing, Peter was standing against the purposes of God for the salvation of the world.

There could be only one source for such an idea, and Jesus recognized it immediately. He rebuked Peter with these unforgettable words: "Get behind me, Satan! You are a stumbling block to me; you do not have in mind the things of God, but the things of men" (verse 23). The rebuke was severe, but it was essential for Peter to know the source of his thoughts.

The rebuke was also part of the preparation that Jesus was putting Peter through for the great calling on his life.

I love the promise that Peter was later able to share with the early Church from his new perspective: "Humble yourselves, therefore, under God's mighty hand, that he may lift you up in due time. Cast all your anxiety on him because he cares for you" (1 Peter 5:6–7). A rebuke from the Lord is an expression of His love and care. We need not fear it or be anxious—it is a sign that He is helping us step into His destiny for us, just as He did with Simon Peter.

I am sorry, Lord, for the times when I have rejected Your loving rebuke in my life. Please forgive me for allowing pride to stand in the way of You pouring out Your heart into mine. I choose to welcome Your rebuke whenever it is necessary. Thank You, Lord, for Your care. In Jesus' name, Amen.

DAY 25

Day 26

FOOLISH THINKING

A fool finds no pleasure in understanding but delights in airing his own opinions.

Proverbs 18:2

A fool takes no interest or pleasure in either the truth that is written in God's Word or the extraordinary evidence all around us of a Creator.

I was recently sitting on a headland, looking out to sea from a Scottish island as the sun slowly sank beneath the distant horizon. I was watching an incredible movie as minute by minute the wind, the waves, the sky and the sun danced to the Creator's baton as He conducted an orchestra of beauty and joy for our pleasure! In my heart I was marveling at the Creator's genius, and at the same time I was weeping because of the fools who see the same scene and have no understanding, but delight in their own opinions.

Science has not produced one shred of evidence to prove that God does not exist, and yet the absence of God from most of the educational curricula of the Western world is powerful evidence that the opinions of atheistic man have now been adopted as fact by an unbelieving world. And once you dispense with the idea of God, you also have to dispense with the laws of God—and right now the world is running headlong toward a catastrophic brick wall, as the consequences of dispensing with the laws of God become the suffering of mankind.

Oh, how God must weep when He sees mankind ignoring all the evidence deducible from His creation! The psalmist got it absolutely right when he said,

> The heavens declare the glory of God; the skies proclaim the work of his hands. Day after day they pour forth speech; night after night they display knowledge. There is no speech or language where their voice is not heard. Their voice goes out into all the earth, their words to the ends of the world.
>
> Psalm 19:1–4

One day there will be a mighty revelation as the Judge of all the earth comes to wind up the universe as we know it. When people see that happening, many will be like the foolish girls in Jesus' parable, rushing here and there trying to get oil in their lamps at the last minute, but it will be too late. For, said Paul,

> since the creation of the world God's invisible qualities—his eternal power and divine nature—have been clearly seen, being understood

from what has been made, so that men are without excuse. . . . Although they claimed to be wise, they became fools.

Romans 1:20, 22

When human pride leads someone to delight in the opinions of man at the expense of believing in Creator God, it is an expression of self-idolatry. And when a person worships his own image, you can be sure that, ultimately, destruction will follow (see Proverbs 16:18).

Thank You, Lord, for the incredible beauty of Your creation. Please forgive us, Lord, for the times when we have preferred to believe the opinions of others, rather than the truth written in Your Word and seen in Your creation. Open my eyes, Lord, to see evidence of You in everything that You have made. In Jesus' name, Amen.

Day 27

CAN YOU BE TRUSTED TO DELIVER GOD'S MESSAGE?

A wicked messenger falls into trouble, but a trustworthy envoy brings healing.

Proverbs 13:17

An envoy carries messages from the one who sends him. He is trusted by his employer to be a faithful carrier of the message, taking it to the person for whom it was intended. An envoy who fails to deliver the message or who distorts the message so that it is no longer the truth will soon be in trouble, will lose his job and, in older days, would probably have lost his life as well! An envoy was trusted to be faithful to the one who sent him.

At the end of Matthew's gospel, Jesus commissioned all His disciples to be His personal envoys and carry the message of the Gospel into all the world. Their role was not only to take the message but to make more disciples, teaching all the new believers to do exactly the same things that He had taught those first disciples to do—which Luke 9:1–2 defines as preaching about the Kingdom of God, healing the sick and setting people free from the powers of darkness.

A trustworthy envoy will not fail to do what he or she has been asked to do, and as the writer of this proverb makes so very clear, the message of a trustworthy envoy will bring healing. And that is exactly what the Great Commission, which Jesus gave to the whole of the Church for the whole of time, does for those who receive the envoys' messages and apply them to their lives.

Salvation is healing. Through the Fall, death entered the human race. This means that we are all, literally, under sentence of death—not just physical death, but eternal spiritual death, total separation from the holy God who created us to love and be loved. When we are saved, we are born again to new life, which means we are raised from the dead (a significant healing!). That means we no longer need fear the physical death that we are all heirs to, for we are already alive in Christ—both for time and eternity.

This is the message that Jesus told His envoys to declare to all who would listen. Then, as we apply the truths of salvation to our lives, God continues to bring His healing and wholeness into every area of our being.

God has entrusted His people to be His envoys, to tell others about the Gospel—not only so that they will become believers, but also that they will become disciples and do the works of the Kingdom. The Great Commission calls us to make disciples—not just believers.

What a privilege it is to be sent by the living God, with the most incredible message that any envoy has ever been given—a message that has the capacity to transform the lives of those who receive and believe it! Are you willing to be a faithful envoy on behalf of the One who has sent you, to be a messenger of His truth and His love to the people Jesus died to save?

Help me, Lord, to be a faithful envoy and never to miss an opportunity to take the message of the Gospel to those who are in need of Your healing and Your salvation. In Jesus' name, Amen.

DAY 27

Day 28

THE HARVEST OF WORK

He who works his land will have abundant food, but he who chases fantasies lacks judgment.

Proverbs 12:11

This proverb comes from the days when each and every family worked their own land in order to grow crops and produce food that would sustain them throughout the year. Land does not produce anything by itself; an abundant harvest requires time and effort. First is preparation of the ground by plowing and nourishing it with manure or other fertilizer. Then it has to be carefully prepared for sowing the seed, followed by regular watering.

All of this represents hard work—but the rewards at harvesttime are great. A farmer who just sowed the seed on unplowed ground, hoping for a good crop, would have very little to harvest at the end of the growing season. His laziness would result in his family going hungry.

Most of us are not able to work land in order to feed our families, but there is still a profound lesson for each and every one of us in today's Scripture. God has given us all gifts and abilities—gifts and abilities that we can use to meet the needs of other people and thereby earn a living. It is no use praying for God to meet our needs if, at the same time, we are failing to work the land of our lives. That is chasing fantasies! Wages never fall off trees; they are earned.

But there is a different kind of harvest about which Jesus was very concerned. We can certainly pray for those individuals in our communities who do not know the Lord, but if we do nothing to plow and nourish the land by building relationships with them, our prayers will be limited in their effectiveness. It was when Jesus met and talked with the woman at the well and shared with her about the water of life that she was changed forever.

A man worked for me for many years. Whenever an opportunity presented itself, I shared with him about the Lord. He became a good friend, but he had seen bad things in wartime, and his heart was hardened toward God. Still, he could not ignore some of the things that God had done in the business I ran. God was preparing him for salvation. I kept plowing his land and sowing good seed.

Then one day he had a heart attack and was critically ill. As I sat with him in his hospital room, he was finally ready to open his heart to God. There was a harvest on earth and rejoicing in heaven that night. The following day he died. Now I am looking forward to seeing him again!

We need to work the land of our lives and always be alert to the potential found in every personal encounter, so that we can plant good seed in the lives of those who are in need of salvation. God has encouraged me in this respect through the words of the prophet Haggai, who said: "'Be strong, all you people of the land,' declares the LORD, 'and work. For I am with you'" (Haggai 2:4).

Help me, Lord, always to use the gifts You have given me to earn the bread that I need for nourishment. But help me, too, Lord, to farm the land of my community and seek to produce a harvest for Your Kingdom—a harvest of lives that have been changed by Your presence and saved for eternity. In Jesus' name, Amen.

DAY 28

Day 29

ALWAYS!

Blessed is the man who always fears the Lord, but he who hardens his heart falls into trouble.

Proverbs 28:14

There are many verses in the Bible that encourage people to live with a holy fear of the Lord, but there is one word in our verse for today that sets this particular Scripture apart from all the others—it is the word *always*.

Always is a word that does not allow for any variation in standard or practice—it simply means, in this context, that whenever you face a choice or a decision in which you have an opportunity either to obey the Lord or to sin, then you do not even have to think about it. The decision in your heart has already been made: You will *always* allow fear of the Lord to determine your actions. The last thing you would ever want to do is grieve the Lord. The peace of God will always follow the decisions you make when they take into account God's perspective before you consider your own—that is what it can mean to fear the Lord.

The second part of the verse explains how it is that people can choose to ignore the Lord and, even though they know something is wrong, go ahead and do it. They have to harden their hearts—and to harden one's heart and go against God is not a good idea. There are many stories in the Bible that tell what happened when people chose knowingly to harden their hearts and oppose God. This happened many times with the people of Israel in their wilderness years after fleeing Egypt.

Hebrews 3:7–11 speaks directly into our own lives, as the writer uses those experiences of the children of Israel to warn us of the dangers of hardening our hearts. When they hardened their hearts, they invoked the anger of God.

And verse 8 in that passage brings us right up to date. This is not a concept that is confined to the history books; it is relevant here and now to teach every one of us, 24/7: "Today, if you hear his voice, do not harden your hearts." Which simply means, when God speaks, listen. And when you have heard, obey!

My great-uncle Will used to say, "Never sit on a spiritual urge," which in his homespun language meant: "What are you waiting for? Get on with it." I have never forgotten him saying those simple but very profound words. And I have always sought to "get on with it" whenever I sensed a spiritual urge from the Lord. I can look back now and say that some of the most important and significant events in my life came about because of doing what Uncle Will taught me. Samuel put it this way when he had to go and correct King Saul: "To obey is better than sacrifice" (1 Samuel 15:22).

A hardened heart is dangerous. Our consciences become dimmed, and we become less and less sensitive to the leading of the Holy Spirit. And the more we go our own way, the harder our hearts become. As today's Scripture warns us, there will be trouble ahead. The word *always* is an antidote to a hardened heart. Allow holy fear to keep your life on God's track, and *always* make your decisions in the fear of the Lord.

Help me, Lord, to remember the importance of the word always. *I recognize that Satan will constantly want to trip me up. I choose now to live in the fear of the Lord and not to harden my heart. Thank You for the promise of the peace of God that will then always be in my heart. In Jesus' name, Amen.*

DAY 29

Day 30

LEARNING LIFE'S LESSONS—
GOD'S WAY

*Train a child in the way he should go, and when he is old he will not
turn from it.*

Proverbs 22:6

Margaret Thatcher was Britain's longest-serving prime minister in the
twentieth century. There will be few reading this who have not heard of
her. The great and famous of the nation, together with Her Majesty the
Queen and the Duke of Edinburgh, were present at St. Paul's Cathedral
for her funeral service.

Margaret Thatcher was known as a strong leader, and she had a deeply
entrenched respect for the laws of God. Where did that come from? It
came from her childhood upbringing. Her father, a Methodist lay preacher,
would take her Sunday by Sunday to churches all over Lincolnshire, where

she heard him preach from the Word of God. God's Word became her childhood meat and drink. While studying chemistry and law at Oxford University, she herself became a Methodist lay preacher. Her sermon "Seek Ye First the Kingdom of God" was described as outstanding. And she took prayer meetings "extremely seriously."

Famous people sometimes have the privilege of preparing the Order of Service for their own funerals. Margaret Thatcher was known for her great attention to detail, so she carefully prepared instructions for how the event should be conducted. She asked specifically that there be no political eulogy at the service, because, she said, "the sole object of worship must be God!"

And then she asked that the prime minister of the day should read the second lesson, chosen by herself from John's gospel. So, at her funeral service, Prime Minister David Cameron read John 14:1–6 to the world, which begins with the words, "Do not let your hearts be troubled. Trust in God," and concludes with Jesus answering Thomas's profound question, "How can we know the way?," by saying, "I am the way and the truth and the life. No one comes to the Father except through me."

So where did this 87-year-old lady learn such wisdom? As our Scripture for the day reminds us, it came from her childhood upbringing. When she became old, she did not depart from what she had learned about God from her father's preaching and her upbringing in the heart of her local Methodist church.

As a child I, too, went with my dad on many occasions when he was preaching at Methodist and other denominational chapels. I sat through

Dad's preaching, and his ministry from the Word of God imperceptibly soaked into my spirit. I was privileged to be blessed in this way.

What a privilege it is for us all to impart the knowledge of God to the next generations! None of us knows what fruit there will be in the generations yet to come. I pray that we will each take seriously our own personal responsibility to impact the generations yet to come with the truth that Jesus is the only way.

Thank You, Lord, for those who have had an impact on my life with truth from the Word of God. Help me, Lord, to serve You and the generations yet to come by sharing my knowledge of You with those who are young, so that when they are old, they will still desire to serve You. In Jesus' name, Amen.

DAY 30

Day 31

WOUNDS THAT BRING HEALING

Wounds from a friend can be trusted, but an enemy multiplies kisses.

Proverbs 27:6

When someone you know, love and trust takes the huge risk of sharing something difficult with you, it may be hard for you to receive and even be hurtful, like a wound. The words may penetrate your defenses and you feel the pain. But such wounds can be life-changing and life-giving, especially when they come from someone with a pure heart and no ulterior motive.

There have been times in my own life when friends with a genuine and rightful concern have come to talk with me—sometimes with a serious issue that I have then had to take to the Lord, and at other times for clarification of something they did not understand. When you know someone's heart, you need not fear his or her motive.

Conversely, when someone flatters you with nice words, especially if they seem over the top, even too good to be true, you are right to be suspicious. Those words could be like the multiplied kisses of an enemy. You begin to suspect an ulterior motive and wonder what that person wants from you. No one likes to be patronized with deceptive words. Proverbs 29:5 expresses it this way: "Whoever flatters his neighbor is spreading a net for his feet."

Because, however, we all like to have nice things said about us, carefully engineered flattery can sometimes make us lower our guard and become vulnerable to serious mistakes. It could potentially trap us into doing something that can have unfortunate, even dangerous, consequences in our lives.

There have been many times when people have come for prayer, but instead of praying with them about their presenting symptoms, I have had to challenge them about something in their lives that was out of order. Often it was something they were trying to hide below the surface but that, in reality, was at the root of their superficial problem. They needed to hear the words of a faithful friend, even though at first it might have felt like a wound.

Sometimes, in circumstances like this, the initial response is anger before they come to the point of recognizing the truth that they need to face. It is not easy to confront people with what are often sensitive issues, but unless you do, you run the danger of missing a golden opportunity to help them get right with God. Proverbs 28:23 neatly sums this up by saying: "He who rebukes a man will in the end gain more favor than he who has a flattering tongue."

When the rich young ruler came to Jesus and asked, "What good thing must I do to get eternal life?" (Matthew 19:16), he might have been expecting a flattering compliment from Jesus for asking such a good question!

But Jesus looked right through him and touched the idol in his heart when He said, "Go, sell your possessions and give to the poor, and you will have treasure in heaven. Then come, follow me" (Matthew 19:21). The reality for this man was that his wealth was more important to him than following Jesus.

Many things can become idols in our hearts. When a friend, in love, has the courage to come and touch that thing, we may be initially angry and feel wounded. But if we open our ears to listen to what God is saying, then such painful encounters can prove to be the most important, most healing days of our lives.

Thank You, Lord, that You care enough about each one of us to confront us with the truth. I pray that, just as You spoke to the rich young ruler, You will speak clearly to me about anything that is out of order in my life. Show me from Your Word or through someone You send to me. Help me not to reject wounds that will bring healing to me, nor to be deceived by flattery. In Jesus' name, Amen.

DAY 31

Day 32

THE POWER OF WISDOM

By wisdom a house is built, and through understanding it is established;
through knowledge its rooms are filled with rare and beautiful treasures.
A wise man has great power, and a man of knowledge increases strength.

Proverbs 24:3–5

Power and authority are not the same thing. A person in authority uses power to carry out whatever it is he or she has to do. A boxer has power in his muscles, but he only has authority to use it in the boxing ring against an opponent. It is the boxing ring that gives him his authority—and it is only here that he can use his power.

Power has the capacity to be a huge blessing or a terrible curse. The power of a railway engine can transport people across the land in comfort. But if that same engine, at the height of its power, leaves the track, there would be a terrible disaster. The power of a wise ruler with a good government can be a huge blessing to the people of a nation. But a despotic ruler who has no other objective than to use his power to control other people and satisfy his own objectives is a curse upon the nations.

Now, the privilege of being the ruler of a nation is reserved for only a few people, but these principles can apply to each and every one of us—for we are all capable of acting with love and generosity toward those who are under our authority or treating them with harshness and cruelty.

I will never forget the woman who almost spat at me when I encouraged her to trust God as her Father. Eventually, through her pain and anger, she told me how her father would beat her and her brothers and sisters every night when he came home from the pub drunk. "I know what fathers are like," she said, "and if that's what God's like, I don't want to know Him!" Her father's wrong use of power in the family had caused her terrible pain and a life of suffering.

Some people use the power they have to inflict suffering on the people they control, so as to make them do what they want out of fear. A harsh boss at work can keep people under control through temper and bad language. And tragically we have prayed in times of ministry with many people who were abused at home, physically, verbally or sexually, by those who wrongfully used the authority that they had in the family.

Our Scripture for today paints a very different picture. It is a picture of a person who has gained knowledge and wisdom in life and, as a result, is making wise and profitable decisions. This individual has become powerful in the community, but only uses that power for good. I will never cease to be thankful to God for wise parents who exercised their authority in the family firmly and with much love. They taught me a great deal, and I will be eternally grateful to them.

The good news for those who have suffered under a harsh authority, wherever that may have been, is that Jesus came to show us what the Father is really like. God is not an abusive Father. His arms of love are always open for the hurting and the broken, for those who have suffered the cruelty of abuse of power. This is the message that God gave through Isaiah to the world (see Isaiah 61:1–3). The Messiah was coming *to heal the brokenhearted and set the captives free.* And there is forgiveness for those who know they have used their powers abusively and cruelly.

Help me, Lord, to forgive those who have abused their power and hurt me at different times of my life. Then help me, Lord, always to use the power that You have given me in every sphere of life with love and wisdom. Help me never to take advantage of those who are under my authority. And thank You, Jesus, that, with all authority given into Your hands, You are still the Good Shepherd who loves and cares for Your sheep—even me! In Jesus' name, Amen.

Day 33

HOW TO PROSPER

Whoever gives heed to instruction prospers, and blessed is he who trusts in the LORD.

Proverbs 16:20

One of the reasons why "pride goes before destruction" (Proverbs 16:18) is that pride tends to make people unteachable. They think they know it all—and they refuse to listen to anyone who tells them what to do or brings any form of instruction or correction into their lives. They know best and that is that!

But, sadly, this means that they can never learn from other people. They condemn themselves to making mistake after mistake because they are never willing to listen to the wisdom of others. This is especially true about learning the ways of the Lord and being willing to listen to His instruction. It is not for nothing that the song "My Way" holds the record for number of weeks—75!—on the U.K.'s Top 40 list. It is also the most requested song for funerals in the U.K. The lyrics, made popular by Frank Sinatra, express supreme arrogance and pride, as they talk about facing the final curtain (presumably death) and saying (presumably to God) that "I did it my way."

Humility is the opposite of pride. And a humble person, who is keen to learn, will grow in knowledge and understanding, learning from others and being equipped for life. A person who loves, respects and listens to the Lord is said to fear the Lord, knowing that what God has said will always be the truth. When we follow Jesus, who is "the way, the truth and the life," then we will be best equipped for living our own lives, whatever the circumstances.

It is no surprise that many places in God's Word encourage us to live our lives in the fear of the Lord. Exodus 20:20, for example, tells us that "the fear of God will be with you to keep you from sinning." My favorite verse about the fear of the Lord is Psalm 25:14, where we read that "the LORD confides in those who fear him."

It is wonderful news to hear that God confides in those who fear Him. That simply means that God will speak directly into our lives by His Spirit or through His Word, showing us what He wants us to do and the way to go.

Isaiah stated it this way: "Your ears will hear a voice behind you, saying, 'This is the way; walk in it'" (Isaiah 30:21). The most costly mistakes I made in my own life were when I decided to ignore God's voice or silence my conscience. The result was always painful. Yes, there is forgiveness for sin, but isn't it—oh! so much—better not to have stepped out of God's way in the first place?

I have seen time and again in my own business life that the most successful and prosperous decisions were those clearly made in obedience to the direction the Lord gave me. Ideas God gave me in specific answer to prayer were the most successful. One business decision I made forty years ago was instrumental in providing financial support for more than thirty years of ministry. God is the best businessman I know, and He delights to confide in us.

When we have learned to trust the Lord, we will not hesitate to be obedient to His Word and do those things that please Him. And, as Proverbs 1:33 expresses it: "Whoever listens to me will live in safety and be at ease, without fear of harm."

Forgive me, Lord, for those times in my life when, through pride, I have tried to do it my way and failed to take wise instruction. Thank You, Lord, that You have promised to guide and direct the steps of those who truly love and fear You. Help me always to be attentive to Your voice and not to wander off the pathway that You lay before me. In Jesus' name, Amen.

DAY 33

Day 34

GUARD YOUR HEART

Above all else, guard your heart, for it is the wellspring of life.

Proverbs 4:23

A wellspring is the place where something important originates. It is the source of a stream and then a river. It is where things begin. And our Scripture for today tells us that the heart is a wellspring, the very center of one's being, the wellspring of life.

The heart being talked of here is not the physical blood pump, but the very core of our being. It is, therefore, absolutely central to who each of us is as a person. It is where our thoughts, feelings and emotions come together and express themselves and influence the choices we make. It is, therefore, of critical importance. No wonder we are told here to guard our hearts—for if we fail to do so, we will be vulnerable to influences from every possible direction and to the temptations the enemy may put before us.

Hebrews 4:12 tells us that it is the thoughts and the attitudes of the heart that are judged by the living and active Word of God, described here as being sharper than any double-edged sword. It is as if the Word of God becomes the straight edge or plumb line against which the choices we make are measured. For when the motives of our hearts are out of tune with God, we are in danger and heading for trouble.

Paul warns us to be very careful what we think about. He encourages us to "take captive every thought to make it obedient to Christ" (2 Corinthians 10:5). The ungodly things we dwell on in our minds penetrate the defenses of our hearts, and we can then become vulnerable to putting those thoughts into action. These actions, in turn, store up ungodly memories for the mind to dwell on, thus feeding a cycle that can dominate and control and become the root of addictions and addictive behavior. This is serious stuff!

How precious it is when children come to faith in Jesus, while still young, before their minds and their hearts have been challenged by the degrading standards that are prevalent in the moral behavior of the adult world. The sooner their hearts are turned toward the Lord, the easier it will be, as they grow and mature, to maintain a pure heart and guard the wellspring of life within them.

Satan wants our hearts to be polluted by ungodly desires. Paul, in his letter to the Philippians, urged believers to counter the enemy's inroads by thinking on "whatever is true, whatever is noble, whatever is right, whatever is pure, whatever is lovely, whatever is admirable" (Philippians 4:8). By so doing, Paul was giving very practical advice on how to guard our hearts as we are urged to do by today's Scripture.

Thank You, Jesus, that with You as the Lord of my life, I can keep my heart pure. Help me to resist the temptations of the enemy and guard my heart, so that Satan is not able to blow my life off course and rob me of my destiny in God. In Jesus' name, Amen.

DAY 34

Day 35

WHAT YOU SEE
IS WHAT YOU GET!

*"For whoever finds me finds life and receives favor from the L*ORD*. But whoever fails to find me harms himself; all who hate me love death."*

Proverbs 8:35–36

WYSIWYG is a popular acronym for *What You See Is What You Get*. Often used in the world of computing to describe the relationship between a display screen and the printed page, it is also used to describe a person whose character is transparent; nothing is hidden. How the person is seen to behave is an exact representation of the true character of the individual. Another way of putting it is that the person is the "same all the way through." Generally, it means that the individual has integrity.

While the acronym WYSIWYG was unknown in Solomon's day, the principle that this acronym stands for was definitely known. Proverbs 6:16–19, for example, lists several things that the Lord hates, three of which are a lying tongue, a heart that devises wicked schemes and a false witness who pours out lies.

People may give the impression that they are pure and truthful. But if in their hearts they are devising evil things, then what is seen on the outside is not the same as what resides on the inside. God hates it when mankind, who was made by God in the image and likeness of our Creator, behaves in a way that is contrary to His character.

But the fact is that every single one of us carries the stain of sin in our hearts—which God hates. In reality, none of us can say that we are one hundred percent WYSIWYGs! Our sin can be forgiven because of what Jesus did for us on the cross, but this side of heaven the sin seed, with all its evil potential, is always there. This is often described as our carnal nature, meaning that we will always fail the WYSIWYG test.

There is only one person of whom this is not true. When Jesus walked this earth, what people saw on the outside was always a true reflection of the inside. He was without sin, and at all times He was a pure, one-hundred-percent-clean representative of His Father, God. The crucial difference between Jesus and every other human being is that, because of sin, all of mankind is under the curse of death. But sinless Jesus was the bringer of life—life in all its fullness.

Only Jesus could say those amazing words from John 14:6: "I am the way and the truth and the life"—for only He is the way to the Father. Only His lips spoke total truth. And only He could be the bringer of life into a world that was under the sentence of death. When people met Jesus, what they saw really was what they got! When they heard Jesus speak, they heard what God the Father would say. John 14:9 quotes Jesus as saying: "Anyone who has seen me has seen the Father."

So, when we read in our Scripture for today that "whoever finds me finds life," we are reading a truth that was vitally important to the people of that day: It speaks of the transparency of godly wisdom. But it also gives a prophetic truth about Jesus that is relevant to us here and now—whoever finds Him, finds life. He is not a deceiver; His teaching will never, ever disappoint; His words will never turn out to be lies; His promises will never let you down. In Jesus what you see is exactly what you get.

> *Thank You, Jesus, that You represented Father God faithfully to a fallen and broken world. Your Word promises that if we truly seek You, we will surely find You. And when we find You, we will find life—resurrection life—life from the dead. Help me never to forget who You are, where You came from and that one day I will be together with You in heaven. In Jesus' name, Amen.*

DAY 35

Day 36

SPIRITUAL LAZINESS

I went past the field of the sluggard, past the vineyard of the man who lacks judgment; thorns had come up everywhere, the ground was covered with weeds, and the stone wall was in ruins. I applied my heart to what I observed and learned a lesson from what I saw: A little sleep, a little slumber, a little folding of the hands to rest—and poverty will come on you like a bandit and scarcity like an armed man.

Proverbs 24:30–34

The Bible is full of parables—from beginning to end. We ignore them at our peril! This one speaks directly to the sin of laziness, and the writer reaches the correct conclusion from what he saw: that the man who sleeps when he should be working will soon end up in poverty. This message is obvious; the advice in the message is lifesaving.

In the working world, we come across many people who are diligent in working for money but careless about the way they live their lives. They know there are issues they need to address, but they have allowed the weeds to grow, and their sensitivity toward the voice of God has been dulled. Their spiritual defenses (the walls of their heart) have been broken down, and oftentimes the enemy has gained access. By responding only to the physical pressures of life, they have ignored the obvious spiritual signs of danger and carried on regardless.

They have said to themselves, *One day, I'll get to it!* But, spiritually, they are behaving like the sluggard in the parable, who never attends to the essentials when caring for his vineyard. Just as surely as the physically lazy person will end up in poverty, the spiritually lazy person will soon become vulnerable—not to armed bandits, but to something much worse. For, as Peter tells us so graphically, "Your enemy the devil prowls around like a roaring lion looking for someone to devour" (1 Peter 5:8).

One of my saddest experiences was listening to the grief of an old man who had known there were things wrong with his life when he was young and had ignored the call of God to love and serve Him. He told himself that he was too busy and too committed to the family business, and that he would answer God's call when he had more time. For now, God would have to wait. In his thirties God spoke to him again. And in his forties and his fifties. But then God ceased to speak.

As an old man, he was heartbroken at his own spiritual laziness, which had robbed him of God's best for his life. He repented and no doubt he received forgiveness—but his life was devoid of the fruit that God had planned for him. God had been robbed also.

Let us not follow the example of the vineyard sluggard but choose now to get out of our spiritual armchairs and tackle any vital issues we have been putting off, before it is too late.

Thank You, Lord, that Your Word reminds me of the need to be diligent in the vineyard of my life. Help me to see where the weeds are growing and the walls are broken down and do something about them without delay. In Jesus' name, Amen.

DAY 36

Day 37

BEWARE THE DANGERS
OF BEER AND WINE

Wine is a mocker and beer is a brawler; whoever is led astray by them is not wise. . . . Do not gaze at wine when it is red, when it sparkles in the cup, when it goes down smoothly! In the end it bites like a snake and poisons like a viper.

Proverbs 20:1; 23:31–32

The argument about whether or not a Christian should drink alcohol has divided believers down through the centuries. It is true that the Bible does not say anywhere that it is a sin to drink alcohol. There is no doubt that Jesus turned the water into the best wine at the wedding banquet. And there are no grounds for thinking that the wine used at the Last Supper was not real wine. But the Bible is also very clear about the inherent dangers of drinking more wine and beer than is good for you. Scriptures such as these cannot be ignored.

No one would dispute that alcohol-fueled behavior is an ungodly curse on society. When people begin to lose control of their tongues and their senses, they become vulnerable to every possible kind of temptation, and their behavior can become obnoxious and aggressive. The courts hear cases constantly of sexual assault and violent behavior driven by the influence of alcohol, wreaking havoc on people's lives and causing terrible suffering. Countless abortions have followed alcohol-inspired sexual activity.

And across the world, driving under the influence of alcohol claims thousands of lives. According to the National Highway Traffic Safety Administration's 2016 traffic safety facts, in the United States alone, thirty people die every single day in motor vehicle crashes that involve an alcohol-impaired driver—that is about eleven thousand deaths a year. This is an astonishing and terrible statistic.

It is not surprising, therefore, that God has placed many warnings in the Bible about the potential spiritual and physical dangers of excessive drinking—we ignore them at our peril. Medical science is now backing up Scripture with well-substantiated health warnings that alcohol consumption can significantly cut life expectancy.

The Bible is making a serious point when it says that in the end, wine "bites like a snake and poisons like a viper." As Christians we should not only listen to these warnings in Scripture but also take note of what medical science is now telling us. The long-term consequences of drinking more than is good for us could be robbing us, our families and God of years of our lives, and also induce years of disease-related suffering. And we should be doubly determined never to touch alcohol if we are about to drive a car.

The bodies God has given us are precious. It is our responsibility to look after them. Paul says, "Do you not know that your body is a temple of the Holy Spirit, who is in you, whom you have received from God? You are not your own; you were bought at a price. Therefore, honor God with your body" (1 Corinthians 6:19).

As believers, we know that everything about our lives is precious to God and that every hour, yes, even every minute, matters to Him. Looking after the body, therefore, is a deeply spiritual responsibility. Today's Scripture should act as an alarm bell to make us review how we treat the bodies God has given us, particularly how much alcohol we consume, so we can remain fit for His service for all the years that God has planned for us.

Thank You, Lord, for the body You have given me and all the things You have created for my enjoyment. Forgive me, Lord, for any way in which I have abused my body by drinking more than is wise. I want to live well all the years You have planned for me. Help me, I pray, to be self-disciplined as I seek to serve You with everything I am. In Jesus' name, Amen.

DAY 37

Day 38

GOD'S RECIPE FOR GOOD HEALTH

Do not be wise in your own eyes; fear the LORD and shun evil. This will bring health to your body and nourishment to your bones.

Proverbs 3:7–8

As we have now discovered, many sayings in the book of Proverbs link the fear of the Lord with godly living. One leads to the other. But this proverb takes the principle a significant step further. It is saying that there can be a definite link between our behavior and our health.

There are three steps to wholeness explicit within these sayings. The first is simply recognition that the wisdom of God is more important than the supposed wisdom of man. Suppose you or I make an assessment of a situation, and our conclusion is different from what God has said in His

Word. If we decide that we know better than God, then we are being wise in our own eyes.

A good example of this in today's amoral world is having sexual relations before marriage. The world says it is okay—and almost everyone does it. Even, sadly, many believers, instead of being salt and light in the world, are bringing the darkness of the world into the Church. Man, supposedly, knows best; and now that we have reliable contraception, they say, "Why not?" This undermines the truth that a man and woman joined together in sex become part of each other; both are now different people than they were before the relationship occurred. If we do not understand this, neither will we have understanding of the consequences of such a union.

It is only fear of the Lord that will keep us from sinning (see Exodus 20:20) and give us the courage and wisdom to avoid evil—not just the thoughts and behaviors that most of us might recognize as evil but, more importantly, the thoughts and behaviors that God defines as evil (sinful) in His Word.

By shunning those things that God defines as evil, we avoid walking in Satan's territory. If you walk through mud, your shoes will carry the stain onto the carpet when you go into your house. If we walk on Satan's turf, we will carry the stain of sin, and sometimes the powers of darkness as well, into our inner being, even our bodies, which should, as described by Paul, serve as "a temple of the Holy Spirit" (1 Corinthians 6:19).

We can now see how our health can be affected by the consequences of not avoiding evil. This helps us understand how it is that sometimes people are physically healed through repentance and deliverance. For when a spirit that has brought infirmity into the body is driven out, then healing can follow—something that I have seen on many occasions as we have prayed for God to deliver and heal. I teach further on these important principles in my book *Healing through Deliverance* (Chosen, 2008). James was very explicit about these matters when he said, "Confess your sins to each other and pray for each other so that you may be healed" (James 5:16).

So, not only is there an eternal spiritual benefit of living a godly life; there is also the temporal physical promise of good health. I am sure that when Solomon wrote today's proverb, he had no idea that blood is made in the bones. The knowledge and wisdom of God are in what he was inspired to write. We read elsewhere in Scripture that life is in the blood (see Leviticus 17:11). With the insights found through medical science, we can more fully understand the significance of these words. Healthy blood leads to a healthy life. If our bones are being nourished, then the whole being is being blessed.

Thank You, Lord, for every detail that You have placed in Your Word. I am sorry for the times when I have not avoided evil, and I have suffered as a result. I pray that You will forgive and cleanse me, so that I may be free to be healed. In Jesus' name, Amen.

DAY 38

Day 39

TRUTH AND INTEGRITY—THE KEYS TO A SUCCESSFUL LIFE

The integrity of the upright guides them, but the unfaithful are destroyed by their duplicity.

Proverbs 11:3

As we come toward the end of our forty-day devotional journey, I would like for us to look at how it is possible to walk into the future with both faith and confidence.

There are key words in today's Scripture—*integrity*, *upright* and *duplicity*. These words will help us understand the principles involved. *Integrity* means that you are the same all the way through. *Upright* means that you choose to live your life according to God's Word and His laws, not your own good ideas. But *duplicity* means being two-faced, dishonest and deceitful.

People who are two-faced are presenting one side of their character to one party and another side to a different party. They can be saying one thing but thinking another. They can be flattering you with their words but despising you in their thoughts.

In terms of our relationship to God, it means that on the outside we are giving the impression that we love the Lord and want to serve Him at all times but that the inner motives of our hearts are very different. We then become unbalanced. It is not surprising, therefore, that a double-minded person is unstable in all his ways (see James 1:8). Unstable and unbalanced people are a danger to themselves and to anyone who chooses to depend on them.

The saddest form of spiritual duplicity is when people swallow their own lies and deceive themselves. They might believe that they are being open and honest, but in reality, the truth of who they are is very different from the image they present. Thus deceived, they use this false image to manipulate others and even try to manipulate God. It is sometimes not easy to see what is going on—even in our own hearts. We need to ask the Holy Spirit to reflect back to us the picture of us that He sees, so that we can become single-minded and not be vulnerable to being imbalanced.

The words *integrity* and *upright* are easier to understand. An upright person is not only one who follows and obeys the Lord, but one whom you can trust not to change in behavior or beliefs to suit the circumstances or a particular audience. A person with integrity is someone you can always trust to be the same in beliefs, reactions and behavior. A person who is upright has integrity; you know that person can be depended on.

That is the sort of person we need to become and remain before God—so that He can always depend on us not only to walk in His ways but also to do His Kingdom works. Then we will not fall into the deadly traps of unfaithfulness caused by duplicity.

It is an exciting but awesome thought: God depends on us to be true to ourselves and true to Him. Throughout Christian history, these are the people on whom God has relied to do His work. They act with integrity and are upright in all their dealings, so God trusts them.

Do you want to be unfaithful, with duplicity as a hallmark of your character? Or do you want to be faithful and live an upright life of truth and integrity? You can be sure that if your heart's desire is the latter, God will rejoice to be at your side to help you in all the stages of life's journey. Proverbs 13:6 tells us that righteousness guards the person of integrity. And Proverbs 4:18 tells us that the path of the righteous is like the morning sun, shining ever brighter till the full light of day.

Thank You, Lord Jesus, that in everything You said and did You acted with truth and integrity, and that, as a result, we can depend on You unconditionally. Help me, Lord, to live with no duplicity in my heart so that You can depend on me always to be available to do whatever You want me to do. In Jesus' name, Amen.

DAY 39

Day 40

"MY WORDS . . . ARE LIFE . . . AND HEALTH"

Listen, my son, accept what I say, and the years of your life will be many. I guide you in the way of wisdom and lead you along straight paths. When you walk, your steps will not be hampered; when you run, you will not stumble. Hold on to instruction, do not let it go; guard it well, for it is your life.

Proverbs 4:10–13

The first few chapters of the book of Proverbs are written as if Wisdom herself is speaking. The name *Wisdom* represents the Holy Spirit of God— for in Him is all truth, all knowledge and all wisdom. We read how Wisdom invites sinful man to learn of God and, through the application of wisdom, to be challenged, encouraged, rebuked, corrected, inspired, healthy, guided and many more things that are expressed through the 31 chapters of this remarkable book.

For this, our final devotion, we come to a very simple instruction—an instruction from Wisdom that, if followed, will have massive consequences for each and every one of us: *Accept what I say.* This is an instruction that can, literally, make the difference between life and death. Do we or do we not believe that what God says is true, and that if we follow and obey Him it will be lifesaving, life-giving and life-fulfilling?

I once saved the life of a terrified young boy whose canoe had capsized in a raging torrent of floodwater. He was stranded on a rock in the middle of the river above a dangerous and very deep dam. I managed to cast my fishing line around his legs, which he took hold of. Then I tied string to the fishing line, and he was able to drag the string to himself. And finally I found a rope in a farmer's barn, which I attached to the string. He grasped the rope and tied it around his waist.

Even though he now had a rope secured around him, the force of the rushing water was too strong for me to be able pull him upstream, away from the dam. To be saved, he was going to have to jump into the raging torrent and trust that I could pull the rope hard and fast enough laterally, across the surface, to prevent him from being sucked under. This danger-ous maneuver would only work if he accepted what I told him to do: Hold on tight to the rope, jump in and trust me.

He did accept what I said. He did trust. And his life was saved. His rescue became a headline in a national newspaper.

The boy had to accept what I said and trust. And that is exactly what Wisdom is saying to us, both in the verses for today and throughout the book of Proverbs. Accept without question that what Wisdom is saying is true and jump into the waters of life, trusting and obeying—for Wisdom says, "I guide you in the way of wisdom and lead you along straight paths. When you walk, your steps will not be hampered; when you run, you will not stumble."

This is extraordinarily good news—these are the rich promises of God to His children. But in order to enjoy the promised blessings, we *must hold on to instruction*. We *must not let it go*. And we *must guard it well*, for it is our life. If the boy in the river had not obeyed the instructions, I could not have saved him. He would have lost his life.

Your life is utterly precious. Jesus died that you might be forgiven and receive a new, born-again life. He has a destiny and a purpose for you. But Satan is a destiny robber; he wants to entice you away from God's best, make you doubt the truth of God's Word and rob you of your life. Follow the advice of Wisdom in the book of Proverbs and God's life-transforming keys will open the doors of opportunity for you.

Today is the first day of the rest of your life. I pray that you will want to follow Him every step of the way.

Thank You, Jesus, for showing me that You are the way to life. Help me, Lord, always to follow the instruction of Wisdom and so enjoy the blessings You have promised in Your Word. I choose now to step into the destiny You have reserved for me by accepting all that You say as the truth and following You all my days. In Jesus' name, Amen.

DAY 40

Peter Horrobin is founder and international director of Ellel Ministries International, which began in 1986 as a ministry of healing in northwest England. The work is now established in more than 35 countries, providing teaching, training and personal ministry opportunities. The American center is in Florida (www.ellel.org/USA).

After graduating from Oxford University with a degree in chemistry, Peter spent a number of years lecturing at the college and university levels, before leaving the academic environment for the world of business. Here he founded a series of successful publishing and bookselling companies.

In his twenties he started to restore a vintage sports car (an Alvis Speed 20) but discovered that its chassis was bent. As he looked at the broken vehicle, wondering if it could ever be repaired, he sensed God asking him a question: *You could restore this broken car, but I can restore broken lives. Which is more important?* It was obvious that broken lives were more important than broken cars, and so the beginning of a vision for healing and restoration was birthed in Peter's heart.

A hallmark of Peter's ministry has been his willingness to step out in faith and see God move to fulfill His promises, often in remarkable ways.

His book *Strands of Destiny* (Sovereign World, 2017) tells many of the amazing stories of what God has done in the past thirty years.

Peter has written and co-written many books including *The Complete Catalogue of British Cars* (Morrow, 1975). And for the past 35 years he has been the co-editor of *Mission Praise* (Harper, 2015), one of the bestselling hymn and songbooks in the U.K. and originally compiled for the visit of Billy Graham in 1984.

In this season of their lives, Peter and his wife, Fiona, are concentrating on writing so that their knowledge and experience can be made permanently available in book form through publishers around the world. His book *Healing through Deliverance* (Chosen, 2008) is now a Christian classic.

More from Peter Horrobin

This 40-day journey of faith explores key verses from the Psalms that David recorded during times of distress, joy and triumph. Within these pages, you will find meditations and prayers to anchor these truths into your own life, and spaces to journal what God is speaking to you. Watch His hand in your life on this journey of discovery and transformation!

Encouragement from the Psalms

What is your heart crying out for? Is it healing from despair, anxiety, anger or chronic illness? In this fortifying book, Peter Horrobin teaches you the basis of faith and helps you learn to walk in deep healing, restoration and freedom. Your struggles will be reshaped into a beautiful story of life transformation by the God who cares zealously for you!

Building on the Rock
Journey to Freedom #1

 **Chosen**

Stay up to date on your favorite books and authors with our free e-newsletters. Sign up today at chosenbooks.com.

 facebook.com/chosenbooks   @chosen_books

 @Chosen_Books